COACHING FOOTBALL'S PRO-WISHBONE ATTACK

COACHING FOOTBALL'S PRO-WISHBONE ATTACK

ROLLIE ROBBINS

with **JIM HALL**

Parker Publishing Company, Inc.
West Nyack, New York

Library of Congress Cataloging in Publication Data

Robbins, Rollie
  Coaching football's pro-wishbone attack.

  Includes index.
    1. Football—Offense. 2. Football coaching.
I. Hall, James Philip,   joint author.
II. Title.
GV951.8.R6   796.33'22   79-25051
ISBN 0-13-139113-5

Printed in the United States of America

How the New Pro-Wishbone Will Help You

This book is a step-by-step plan for a new offense that features the explosive ball-control option attack of the Wishbone, the quick-hitting, secure outside handoff run attack, plus the quick-scoring threat of a versatile pro passing game. It is a potent, multi-weapon offense that assures both ball control and the ability to burst into the end zone quickly and often.

This new offense is called the "Pro-Wishbone" or "Pro-Bone." The offense features one basic backfield set, which facilitates the execution of precise fundamentals necessary to the development of an explosive offensive package. It works for the coach who wants a thorough plan to institute an exciting system, designed to achieve high scoring results even with average talent.

This book is the first one to be written about this new and innovative offense. The Pro-Bone offers ball control and catch-up football, run from the same set, learned from the same system. The power off-tackle plays and the end sweeps, essential to the establishment of a sound running game, are present. One-on-one blocking, set up with appropriate line spacing, gives defensive linemen a different look on each play. The resulting uncertainty of the linemen, plus a number of other factors, opens up the running game. Defensive backs are forced to play further from the line of scrimmage, due to the deep pass threat. Linebackers are frozen by the faking back. Five options are present on every play. The quickness of the fullback keeps the middle defense frozen while the quarterback carries out his faking. One back is always running counter backfield motion, which cuts down defensive pursuit and aids breakaway play action.

The Pro-Bone presents a formidable challenge to opposing teams. Here are the specific characteristics of the Pro-Bone, that spell out just how formidable that challenge is:

1. *Excellent blocking angles*: Each of the offensive plays can be run from three variable line spacings. In short spacing, the guards are 1 foot from the center, the tackles are 2 feet from the guards, and the tight end is 3 feet from the tackle. In regular spacing, the guards are 2 feet from the center, the tackles are 4 feet from the guards, and the tight end is 9 feet from the tackle. In wide spacing, the guards are 3 to 4 feet from the center, the tackles 6 feet from the guards, and the tight end is 12 feet from the tackle. This type of spacing keeps the offensive linemen from having to block head-on each play. The line spacing doesn't alter the backfield spacing, and hence the quarterback's timing with his handoffs is not affected. The pressure to line up properly rests with the defense.

Linemen can be taught three basic blocking techniques: the butt block, the cut-off block and the reverse crab block. Simplifying the line blocking enables the offense to use a quick count cadence, a broken cadence, a silent count and audibles on the line of scrimmage. The line blocking proceeds from the count-off blocking system.

2. *Backfield action stops defensive pursuit*: The fullback lines up very close to the line of scrimmage, and, on the Pro-Bone option, runs away from the area where the quarterback and halfbacks will be running. The quickness of the fullback from his short distance from the line of scrimmage makes the linebackers play the fullback on every play. Thus, defensive linemen and linebackers cannot key on the fullback or halfbacks because of the counter action.

3. *Easy option reads for the quarterback*: In reverse pivoting to the fullback, whether the quarterback gives or fakes depends on the defensive alignment. His second read comes from seeing if the defensive tackle is driven off the line of scrimmage. The third read

tells whether the defensive end comes for him or drops off the line of scrimmage—the regular defensive end option read—whether to keep or pitch. The fourth read comes from the defensive alignment as it is seen by the quarterback from the start position, looking for such things as a tight end not being covered downfield.

4. *Wide running lanes*: Wider running lanes are created by the counter action of the fullback. Backs are running to areas that are not congested with other backs and linemen. The wide spacing that can be used by the offensive line also opens up wider running lanes. The wider lanes create more one-on-one situations for the backs, and they lead to more yardage.

5. *Versatile offensive sets*: Every play is started from the basic option set. The regular set, motion set, overload set, plus every passing series of the Pro-Bone, all look the same to the defense when the offense lines up. This vastly simplifies the quarterback's tasks. His backs will be coming from the same distance and from the same position each time. Valuable time is saved that would otherwise have been spent teaching backs the different positions necessary for different offensive series.

This book will facilitate rapid implementation of the Pro-Wishbone. Since any coach who implements a new offense must organize himself and his staff toward the new system's objectives, each chapter is designed to help clarify the philosophy behind the organization of drills and practice sessions, as well as to establish basic terminology.

The theme is simplicity. The offensive concepts are made understandable by delineating them one sequential step at a time, incorporating technical coaching points as well as organization— from plans for the first practice to the installation of the Pro-Bone in a game situation.

This is the book for a coach who can't spend an entire season teaching a lineman how to arrange his stance. Few coaches have the time or the staff to do this. The Pro-Bone is flexible and adaptable, and, as will be seen, it doesn't require super athletes. Depending on a given school's situation, a coach could stay with the basic option or use as many of the multi-formations from the basic option as seem feasible.

Thus, the Pro-Bone offers: explosiveness, the ability to score quickly and often, ball control, multi-formations, the basic Wishbone option, quick-hitting handoff offense, power blocking, explosive pro passing attack, a quick outside attack, no pursuit defense, and finally, all of the above are easy to coach and teach.

Rollie Robbins
Jim Hall

COACHING FOOTBALL'S PRO-WISHBONE ATTACK

Contents

9. Effective Pro-Bone Play Selection for Specific Defenses 189

1

Advantages and Design
of the Pro-Bone

The Pro-Bone came into being because of problems associated with other systems. The Wishbone, I, Power I and Pro-Set provide either a good running attack or a good passing attack. The Wishbone and Veer provide adequate fake run pass options, but not the deep pass without change of formation. In the face of these problems, many coaches have gone to multiple-set offenses for more balance, hoping to cause adjustment problems for opposing defenses.

THE BASIC OPTION SET

The Pro-Bone consolidates the advantages of all these systems into one basic option set. This basic set splits the halfbacks wide for run and pass routes. The fullback is set very close to the quarterback, demanding that the defense respect the inside power running game. The line varies position to aid the running backs and to protect the quarterback when he passes. In addition to its strategic strengths, the Pro-Bone is easy to teach, adapting itself well to available talent at the high school and college level.

Diagram 1-1 shows the basic Pro-Bone set. A close look at it will reveal how the concepts described above are put to use.

Notice that the line set is typical Pro-Set/Veer/I, including the arrangement of the split end and the tight end. Notice, however, that the fullback is located only 1 yard behind the quarterback. From here, the fullback hits holes quickly and is in position for good angle blocking. The fullback is so close to the line of scrimmage that the

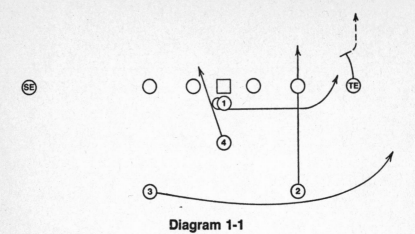

Diagram 1-1

linebacker must stay home. Further complicating things for the defense, the basic option play always begins with the fullback running counter action to the rest of the running backs. The fullback always runs off the reads of the blocking guards and center.

The quarterback reads where the fullback will be running when he comes to the line of scrimmage. The handoff to the fullback is easy, requiring only a reverse pivot back to the line of scrimmage.

Halfbacks align themselves behind the tackles. The positions of the latter are determined by the line spacing required for a given play—short, regular, or wide spacing. The distance from halfback to quarterback is always the same, 4½ yards, which provides time to mesh properly and to read the defensive tackle.

The design of the offense is easy to teach and to learn. The offense *is* simple, but, as will be seen, offensive lightning is possible on every snap.

Looking at the basic Pro-Bone set, you see that the offense can be changed by motion, without changing blocking assignments or backfield alignment. The assignments for the backs remain the same, whether motion is used or not, so backfield positions are easy to learn. It is easy for one back to learn another back's position, which can be a definite plus when depth is a problem.

Diagram 1-2 makes this clear: On the 36 Sweep, the two back is motioned right. The motion does not alter the blocking (and, hence, the potential effectiveness) of the play. But the pass threat is greatly increased, with the motion back becoming a potent receiver as he overloads a particular area. If the defense does not adjust to the

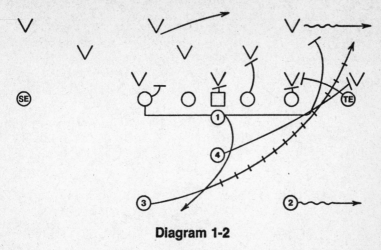

Diagram 1-2

motion, the quarterback can change the play on the line of scrimmage and pass.

ADAPTABILITY OF THE OFFENSE

The Pro-Bone adapts itself well to the personnel you have available. If, for example, you have a small fullback, the quickness of the smaller man can be used on quick dives up the middle. If you do not have the super option quarterback, the power offense can be run, in which the quarterback's primary function is to hand off to the running backs. The three back position is the place for the great running back, should the latter be available.

If you do have a super quarterback, the Pro-Bone allows for motion by the fullback, who then becomes another receiver. The defense must cover the fullback on the original set, so again it is forced to adjust when the fullback goes in motion. See Diagram 1-3.

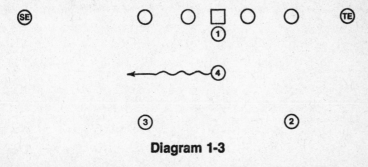

Diagram 1-3

These small changes in the offense, requiring adjustments by the defense, point up the ways that the offense can be adapted to your specific needs. You can give the offense any stamp you wish, yet start each play from the one basic set. Furthermore, your specific personnel can be utilized to the best of their ability.

ADVANTAGES OF THIS OFFENSE

Here are the specific advantages of the Pro-Bone's five-option offense:

1) Every series and play begins from the same basic option set.
2) The quarterback has five options on every play.
3) Every series is run with the same count-off blocking for the line.
4) The option reads for the quarterback are easy to teach and learn.
5) The counter backfield action of the fullback stops defensive pursuit.
6) A pass threat exists on every play.
7) Rollout or dropback passing can be utilized, according to coaching preference or quarterback ability.
8) The offense is effective for both ball control and catch-up.
9) Running lanes are wide, due to line and back spacing.

Look again at the basic Pro-Bone set in Diagram 1-4. The fullback has the counter action mentioned above, and can hit the line of scrimmage quickly.

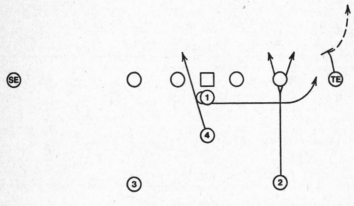

Diagram 1-4

The fullback's positioning gives him excellent blocking angles. As we mentioned previously, the fullback's position in the Pro-Bone can be occupied by a number of types. He needn't, in other words, be a bruising back in the Larry Csonka mold. A smaller, quicker person can be used, and used effectively. (See Diagram 1-5.)

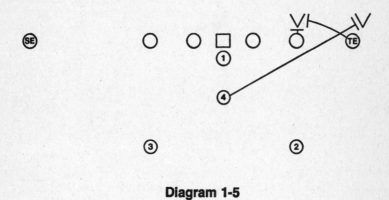

Diagram 1-5

The halfbacks are set so that they can get outside positioning quickly. (See Diagram 1-6.)

When the backs are in the basic set, lead blocking is used in power plays. (See Diagrams 1-7 and 1-8.)

Beside the blocking and spacing advantages of the Pro-Bone, the defense must prepare to cover five possibilities on every play:

1) The fullback could get the ball.
2) The halfback could get the ball.
3) The quarterback could keep.
4) The quarterback could pitch outside to the halfback, who is in excellent position.
5) The quarterback could throw an easy pass to the tight end.

The objectives of the Pro-Bone are to 1) utilize available personnel effectively, 2) keep the defense adjusting to the offense, 3) keep the defense from good pursuit angles, 4) create offensive imbalance by putting an additional blocker in an offensive zone, and 5) provide versatility.

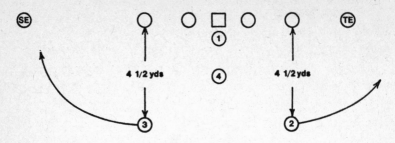

Diagram 1-6

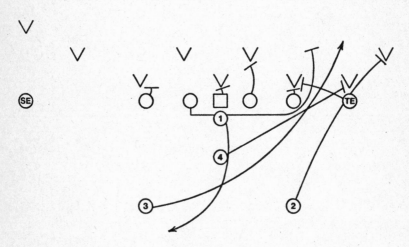

Diagram 1-7

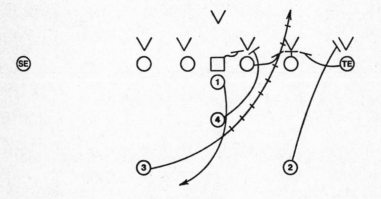

Diagram 1-8

The Pro-Bone has the above, plus quick-scoring potential and, should the situation demand it, ball control capability. The offense is easy to install and fun to run, and can be used by any size coaching staff with success.

2

Coaching the Pro-Bone

UTILIZING PERSONNEL

The Pro-Bone utilizes personnel effectively. High schools especially, year in and year out, cannot count on an abundance of super athletes. Although skilled athletes can be employed at key positions to maximum advantage in the Pro-Bone, the simplicity of line blocking and offensive back routes, plus the variety of spacings and blocking assignments for linemen and backs, provide for the effective use of all available personnel. Diagram 2-1 again shows the basic offensive set.

While it is understood that you will have your own criteria, here are some general considerations to be kept in mind when assigning personnel to various positions. (A first consideration could be to time each member of the squad in the 40-yard dash.)

Tight End

The tight end's primary responsibility is to block. With the tackle, the tight end does the seal blocking for sweeps. He must also

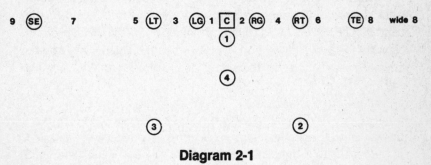

Diagram 2-1

be able to block down on the inside linebacker. It may be best to look for tackle-types who are quick and who can learn to catch the football. Basketball centers and forwards tend to make good tight ends.

Strongside Tackle

The RT is generally the largest lineman. He must be able to block straight ahead, keeping the defensive man from penetrating.

Right Guard

The RG must be a good straight-ahead blocker. His main function is standoff blocking and cross blocking.

Center

The center must be able to snap the ball for punts and extra points, as well as deliver the ball consistently to the QB. Talented high school players can be reminded of the priority placed on this position by college recruiters.

Left Guard

The LG must be quick, because he does most of the trap blocking and pulling on sweeps. Both guards should be helped to develop pulling skills and quickness, but the LG should be the better athlete.

Left Tackle

The LT is the quicker of the tackles, perhaps even a guard-type player. He pulls on the quick pitch left, and seals down when the guard pulls.

Four Back (Fullback)

In the Pro-Bone, the four or fullback should be a hard-nosed football player who can block and run. Size is secondary, since most blocking will be good-angle blocking. Since the FB is so close to the QB, a quick start is helpful.

Two Back (Halfback)

While it would be desirable to have skilled athletes at all backfield positions, the two back position does not absolutely demand it. The three back is usually groomed at the two back position. Right halfbacks can have good games when the defense keys on the three back—pointing up the fact that the Pro-Bone does not key well.

Three Back (Halfback)

The three or left halfback is the best running back. He runs the strongside sweep and leads the weakside sweep. The latter is the SE side when double tight ends are used. The three back runs quick pitches and is the release man on three-man pass patterns.

Quarterback

The QB is usually the best athlete on the squad. The best junior high athletes should be groomed as quarterbacks. Playing option football at the quarterback position requires a variety of skills, and the sooner training begins, the better.

Split End

The SE should be one of the fastest men on the squad. He should have good hands and the ability to block and run disciplined pass routes.

This short position sketch is provided only as a guide for new coaches who may wish to use a scale system to position their athletes. The Pro-Bone can be personalized to fit any coach's individual preferences in regard to personnel. The position sketch may also clarify the following material on line and back spacing, which is necessary to an understanding of the basic option play.

LINE SPACING

An advantage of the Pro-Bone is its incorporation of varied line spacing. This helps to isolate the defensive player and keep him from penetrating into running lanes. Varied spacing is possible because of the depth and width of the offensive backs. Diagram 2-2 illustrates the *regular split,* the *wide split* is seen in Diagram 2-3, and the *short split* is shown in Diagram 2-4. These are the three basic types of spacing.

The first advantage of the different spacings is that the defense must determine its alignment on each play. This creates the second advantage, which is the greater possibility that defensive players

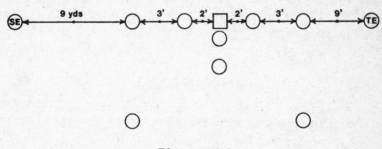

Diagram 2-2

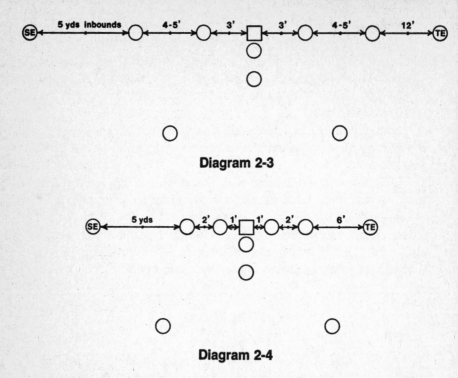

Diagram 2-3

Diagram 2-4

will be out of position. Possibilities increase for mistakes in defensive coverage.

These advantages, along with the offensive linemen knowing the snap count, lead to greater chances for picking up good yardage. Additionally, the different line spacings let the QB have a better read on the defense, with less chance for defensive realignment before the ball is snapped.

The different splits allow you to make optimum use of offensive personnel. If linemen are quick, splits can be adjusted out; if linemen are slower, short splits can be used more often. Line spacing calls will be discussed—in terms of specific plays and field position—in Chapter 7.

BACK SPACING

Back spacing is shown in Diagram 2-5. The depth of the backs makes it easy for both the QB read and the HB read cutting off the block of the tackle.

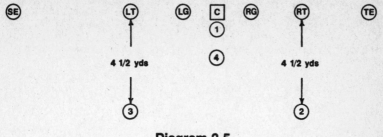

Diagram 2-5

When the line spacing changes, the back spacing remains the same. Halfbacks are lined up behind the tackle. The wide spacing will leave the backs inside the tackles, with their helmets on the inside of the inside hip of the tackles.

The depth of the backs can be adjusted depending on the personnel available. Backs should be timed in 5-yard sprints as well as in the 40-yard dash. Some backs have quicker starts, which wouldn't necessarily show up in the longer sprint.

Such is the preliminary information on line and back spacing. Tight end and split end splits are also important, but that information will be better understood after a discussion of the heart of the Pro-Bone, the basic option play.

THE BASIC OPTION PLAY

The QB is the key to the option. His getting to the halfback is the critical phase of the play. As shown in previous diagrams, the FB is very close to the QB—2 to 3 feet behind him. The QB will show the ball to the FB and then continue the reverse pivot down the line left or right, depending on the option call. See Diagram 2-6.

Since the play is so important, we should go through it step by step:

1. The QB receives the ball from the center and pivots on his left foot. The right foot is placed parallel to the left foot, shoulders-width apart.

2. Holding the ball in both hands, the QB places the ball in the fullback's stomach. The FB comes over the ball, but does not take it unless he has been named as the designated ball carrier, or feels the ball left by the QB. The FB should be coming toward the line of scrimmage, head up, looking at the blocking of the offensive guard in front of him. Considerable time should be spent

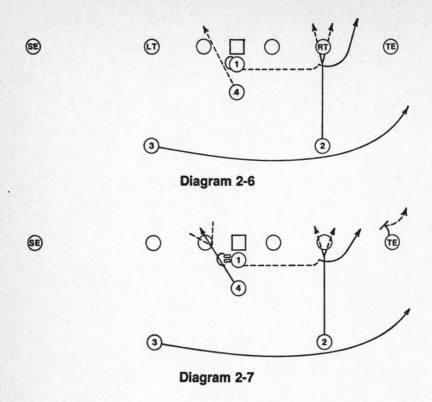

Diagram 2-6

Diagram 2-7

teaching the FB to read the guard's block. The QB must get the FB read from the line of scrimmage when he first comes over the ball. The QB signal call will be dealt with in Chapter 7.

3. From the parallel foot position, the QB pivots on the right foot, extends the left foot down toward the two back, stays parallel to the line of scrimmage, and does not give ground (Diagram 2-7).

4. The QB engages the two back as in a regular option, reading the defensive tackle. The defensive end is blocked by the TE, giving the QB time to get from the FB to the two back. The QB rides with the two back for a step or two. The handoff depends on the DT. If he is blocked, the QB hands off, and if he is not, the QB keeps. The two back reads the block of the tackle as to the cut he will take. Drills for reads for each position will be covered in Chapter 8.

5. The QB then options the outside defensive end. If he keeps the ball, he cuts upfield. If he sees that the TE is not covered by the defensive halfback, he may throw a pass for the TE to run under. If the QB keeps, he should cut directly upfield and get as much

yardage as possible. The key for the QB is the outside defensive end or corner.

6. When the QB is covered by the outside CB, he may pitch to the three back, who is 5 to 7 yards deep.

EXECUTING THE READ

At first glance, this can seem like a lot of option to carry out. The reads for the QB, however, are surprisingly easy. He is not pressured by long rides and pitches in which he is not in direct eye contact with the flare halfback, as in the regular Wishbone outside option. In fact, the QB can call who will carry, without hurting the five-option possibility. Possibilities include Option Right Second Man, Outside Pitch Right, Option Right Fullback, Option Right Keep, and Option Right Pass TE. Further simplification is provided by the depth of the three back flare running pattern where the QB has good eye contact for the pitch.

MESH TIMING

When the QB is turning to hand off to the FB on the start of the Option Right, the guard splits dictate to the FB read that when the guards are split wide, the FB can run off the blocking of the guard. The wide split of the guard helps the FB to see where the defensive linemen and linebackers are located.

The QB, in handing off to the FB, reverse pivots, facing hin directly. The FB runs directly toward him and veers left or right depending on the option that is called.

When the splits of the guards are short, the FB's route will be to the outside hip of the offensive guard. The FB should always be heading upfield, never parallel to the line of scrimmage.

If the defense is a gap defense, the line will always block down to the gap. The FB must run directly toward the blocking guard, using his momentum to break into the secondary.

The reverse pivot of the QB is a continuous motion, which keeps momentum going down the line of scrimmage to the mesh point with the HB. The closeness of the FB permits this kind of action by the QB. The closeness of the FB also gives the QB time to reach a good mesh point with the HB in terms of the read on the tackle.

The mesh point of the QB and HB is not affected by the splits of the line. By looking at Diagrams 2-10, 2-11, and 2-12, you can see that the HB is always the same distance from the QB, so the timing remains the same.

The wide splits of the tackles create wide running lanes or a good block down situation. The HB can cut outside or make it possible for the QB to cut upfield from him.

REASONING BEHIND THE FIVE-OPTION OFFENSE

With a good read each time, the option calls can take the pressure off the new QB until he learns the offense. Once the QB has mastered the option, he can make a call, then change the call, either at the line of scrimmage or on the exchange during the handoff. The problem of a young QB having full responsibility for hard reads, whether to keep or hand off, is alleviated. The QB can easily read the defensive line close to him and have immediate pressure from the defensive tackle or end. The tackle blocking the DT keeps the defensive man off the line, and the TE hitting the man over him also provides more time.

If the DE and the CB do come hard, the pass to the TE opens up. The QB can throw right after the fake to the two back, depending on the option called. The throw is from the position shown in Diagram 2-8. The outside flare man should block the first man to the outside, and the dive back should block on the line of scrimmage.

The Option Left is the mirrored opposite of the Option Right. In the Option Left, the FB is blocking on the line of scrimmage and the dive back is back, giving the QB more protection. This makes it

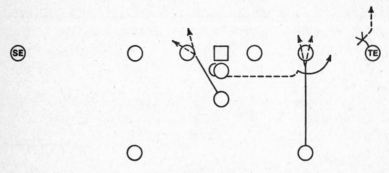

Diagram 2-8

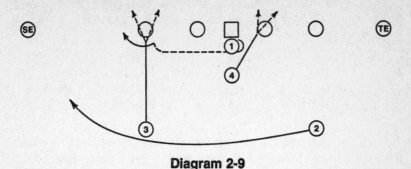

Diagram 2-9

more difficult for the defense to read pass blocking. See Diagram 2-9.

The Option Left has these variations from the Option Right:

1. The QB pivots on his right foot instead of his left.
2. The FB comes by on the QB's right.
3. After reaching the parallel foot position, the QB pivots on his left foot and extends his right foot toward the three back.
4. The QB engages the three back, reading this time the defensive corner (the SE can flex to keep the CB off the line).
5. If the QB reads that the three back run is open, he hands off. If not, he carries out his options as described for the Option Right.
6. A pass to the SE is the other possibility.

In addition to the line spacing and back spacing changes outlined earlier, there are variations in pass blocking. These will be discussed in Chapters 5 and 7.

TIGHT END AND SPLIT END SPLITS

Flanker and TE splits can be changed to make the defense keep changing position. Whenever the defense must check alignment, it helps to break their defensive key concentration and increases the odds that a mistake will be made in defensive alignment.

The SE can be adjusted from double tight end, to 5 yards out, to the normal 10 yards out, to 5 yards inside the out-of-bounds marker. These adjustments go with the 60 motion series, 70 flanker series, and sweep passes.

The regular position for the TE is a 3-yard split. This keeps the defensive man with him. To create a different offensive look, he can be split to 6 yards, causing the defense to drop off the line of scrimmage.

A last reminder about spacing: Changed spacing of the linemen does not alter the positioning of the offensive backs. The position changes of the linemen help to create running lanes for the backs. See Diagrams 2-10 (regular spacing), 2-11 (short spacing), and 2-12 (wide spacing).

The only alignment change for the backs would involve moving them closer to the line of scrimmage if they are too slow for the second option. Their depth helps them to come straight ahead, head up, reading the block of the offensive tackle.

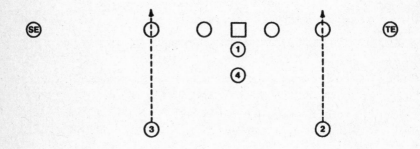

Diagram 2-10

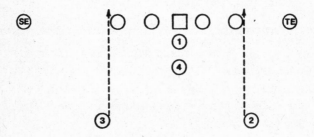

Diagram 2-11

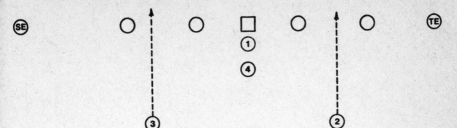

Diagram 2-12

3

Developing Versatile
Pro-Bone Options

As we said earlier, the Pro-Bone came into being because of numerous problems associated with other offensive systems. The Wishbone, I, Power I and Pro-Set each provide what is primarily either a good running or passing attack. The Wishbone and Veer provide adequate fake run pass options, but not the deep pass without a change of formation. Because these formations lack the necessary versatility, coaches have gone to multiple-set systems for balance.

The Pro-Bone's versatility—from one set—is its key advantage. Its plays can be conveniently divided into five sections: the basic option series; power plays, including sweeps; counters, crossbucks and reverses; plays using motion; and specialty plays.

Again, all of these plays are run from the same basic option set. It must be remembered that, when defensing a given offense, you must be concerned with the most serious threat of that offense. If an offense must change formation to run power plays or counters—or to pass—then the defense can make appropriate changes and key. Since the Pro-Bone set is the same for all plays, the disadvantage for the defense is clear.

Here then are the basic plays, in the five divisions as outlined above. A position analysis is included to help you to select appropriate personnel. We will spend considerable time on the basic option plays, as they are the heart of the offense.

Since the option is the key to the offense, most teams trying to defense the Pro-Bone put a high priority on stopping the option plays. One difficulty with this, however, is that the Pro-Bone doesn't have three options going in the same direction; the fullback counter action is away from the defensive flow. Another is that the tight end going downfield keeps the defensive half from coming up and forcing.

Many teams defense the Pro-Bone with the 5-2 Okie Defense because of the Pro-Bone's similarity—in appearance—to the Wishbone. Some use the 5-2 Monster to the tight end side. The odd man in front of the five-man defensive line permits the offense to outnumber the defense on the line of scrimmage. See Diagram 3-1.

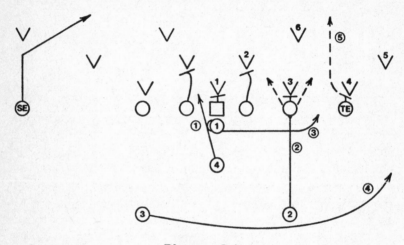

Diagram 3-1

Should any of the backs break into the secondary, they will likely find themselves in a one-on-one situation with a defender, which makes for longer yardage plays. Pursuit is cut down.

Diagram 3-2 shows the passing advantages of the Pro-Bone against the 5-2 Monster, primarily the ability to throw back to the weak side.

It bears repeating that the balanced effect of the backfield—with the halfbacks as wide and deep as they are—keeps the defense spread. The short distance of the fullback from the line of scrimmage keeps the linebackers from pursuing.

With this preamble about how teams defense it, let's look at the basic option plays. Diagrams 3-3 and 3-4 show the basic option against even and odd defensive fronts.

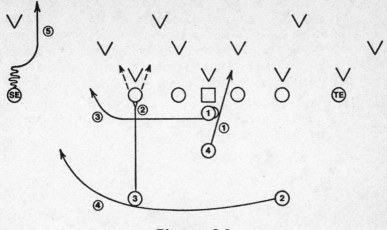

Diagram 3-2

BASIC OPTION LEFT AND RIGHT

Option Right (Diagram 3-3—Even, Diagram 3-4—Odd)

SE: Runs 10-yard sprint post pattern.

LT: Hits man outside, releases for downfield blocking.

LG: Hits man over him or immediate LB. FB will cut-off block.

C: Hits man over him or immediate LB (cut-off blocking).

RG: Hits man over him or immediate LB (hit drive and crab cut-off block).

RT: Hits man over him or to inside (drive block, taking the man off the line of scrimmage), then cuts off with reverse crab block.

TE: Hits man over him, then releases downfield to block.

QB: Calls type of line split in huddle, checks defense on line of scrimmage for handoff to FB. Makes quick reverse pivot read on FB. Continues reverse pivot down the line of scrimmage, reads the HB, makes good fake. If he does not hand off, he pulls the ball in immediately and gets ready for the option on the end. Any time the defense comes up quickly, QB throws option right pass to the tight end.

FB: Reads the defensive guard as to whether to run inside or outside. Carries fake out 8 yards, then looks for downfield blocking.

RH: Reads the defensive tackle to see how he will be blocked. Keeps his head up, looking to see how the OT is blocking. Keeps an open pocket for the QB to put the ball into. If given the ball, he tries to keep it hidden, and breaks toward open running room. If not given the ball, he carries fake out 8 yards, then looks to block first man downfield.

LH: Steps right, stays deep, watching for the pitch from the QB. If the ball is pitched, LH must watch it into his hands, then start running to open field, trying to pick up blockers.

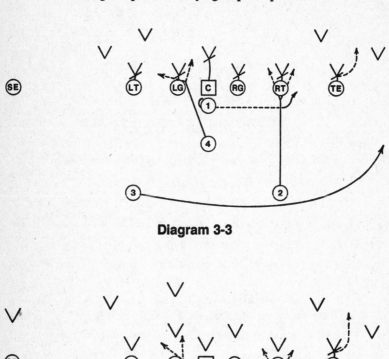

Diagram 3-3

Diagram 3-4

Option Right Pass

The Option Right Pass, seen in Diagram 3-5, is run the same way, except that the two back starts toward the hole, then veers to the right and blocks the first man.

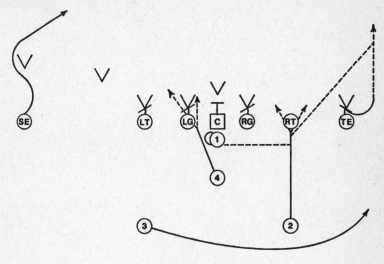

Diagram 3-5

Option Left

Option Left is a mirror of Option Right, with the exceptions noted. See Diagrams 3-6 (regular split—even) and 3-7 (odd).

SE: Sprints toward defensive HB, hits him chest high with good block. After the block, SE continues downfield on flag pattern. If the DH follows, SE runs a 10-yard in and flag pattern.

LT: Blocks man over or to inside (drive block, taking the man off the line of scrimmage, then cutting him off with reverse crab block).

LG: Blocks man over or immediate LB. Hits, makes drive and crab block between himself and ball carrier.

C: Blocks man over or immediate LB (cut-off block).

RG: Blocks man over or immediate LB. FB runs off block.

RT: Blocks man to outside, releases downfield to block.

TE: Brushes man and goes downfield to cut off pursuit.

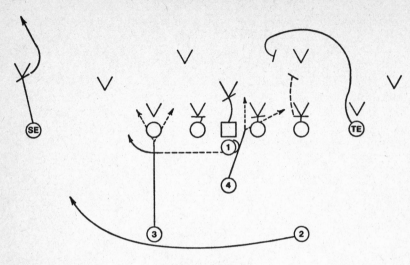

Diagram 3-6

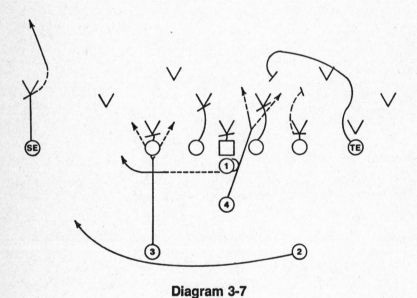

Diagram 3-7

QB: Calls type of line splits in huddle, checks defense on line of scrimmage for type of handoff to FB. Reverse pivots to his right, fakes or hands off to FB, continues pivot, stays parallel to the line of scrimmage. Reads the LH, making sure the fake is good. If he does not hand off, he pulls the ball in immediately and gets ready for the option on the end. The QB should take as much ground on the option as he can. Any time the LB or the DE come up fast, the QB should throw the Option Left Pass to the SE. If the ball is pitched to the two back, he should make sure that the pitch is soft and in front of him.

FB: Reads DG as to whether to run inside or outside. Carries fake out 8 yards, then looks for a downfield block.

LH: Reads DT to see how he is being blocked. Keeps head up, keeps pocket open for the ball. If given the ball, keeps it hidden, breaks toward open running room.

RH: Steps left, stays deep, looks for pitch from QB. If the ball is pitched, RH watches it into his hands, then runs to open field, paying attention to the block of the TE.

Option Left Pass

The Option Left Pass (Diagram 3-8) is run the same way, except that the three back starts toward the hole, then veers to the left and blocks the first man.

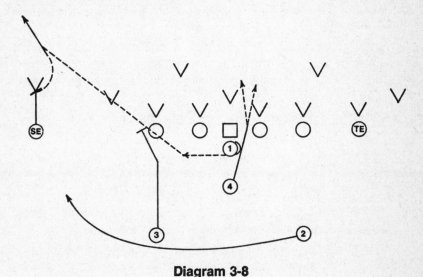

Diagram 3-8

POWER PLAYS

The second series of plays has to do with power plays. Because of the positioning of the fullback, the Pro-Bone lends itself extremely well to power running. This is a key aspect of the Pro-Bone's versatility. Since the fullback provides for excellent short yardage plays, defenses must prepare during the week for this kind of offensive action.

The bread-and-butter plays of the power series are the sweeps and power leads. Before describing the plays themselves, let's discuss some keys to their success.

On Sweeps 36 and 25, one key is the double-team blocking of the tight end and tackle. The tackle has to drive the defensive tackle off the line of scrimmage. He should do this with a crab block straight into the man, head very low, driving him straight back. The tight end seals the tackle from the outside.

The reason that the defensive tackle must be moved off the line of scrimmage is to cut off inside pursuit by the linebacker. Should the defensive man charge so low that he meets the tackle head on, the tackle should take a check step with his right foot, drop his shoulder and headgear, and try to go underneath the defensive man.

The offensive tackle must meet the charge of the defensive man first and stop his momentum. The tight end then attacks the highest part of the defensive man's body and rolls him over.

The tackle usually will not meet a defensive tackle in this bury position because the offense is set up to run the option, and the defensive man, to play the option correctly, cannot charge this way.

SWEEPS LEFT AND RIGHT

Sweep plays are shown in Diagrams 3-9 through 3-16.

Sweep 36 (Diagram 3-9—Even, Diagram 3-10—Odd)

SE: Runs 10-yard sprint post pattern. On plays like this, SE should be testing for potential open patterns.

LT: Blocks down on first man to inside, making sure DG does not follow pulling guard. Makes sure shooting LB does not get through.

LG: Pulls right, staying tight to the line of scrimmage. Cuts up through hole and blocks first man through hole.

C: Blocks man over him or immediate LB. Makes cut-off block after original contact.

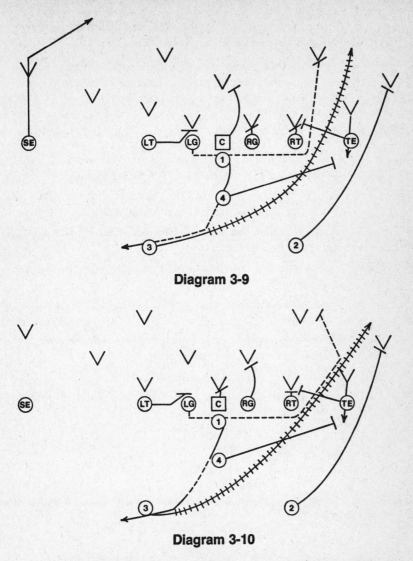

Diagram 3-9

Diagram 3-10

RG: Blocks man on line or immediate LB. Makes cut-off block after original contact.

RT: Makes drive block on defensive man's legs, setting up double-team leg TE.

TE: Blocks down on the DT, sealing the inside.

QB: Reverse pivots, hands off deep to three back. Fakes QB keeper pass to SE.

FB: Drives hard toward DE or first loose man to the outside. Drive blocks man backward, then goes to cut-off block.

RH: Sprints hard to outside and blocks defensive corner or HB.

LH: Steps forward, then heads toward hole. When handed the ball, moves right hard and follows blocking.

Wide Sweep 38 (Diagram 3-11—Even, Diagram 3-12—Odd)

SE: Runs 10-yard sprint pattern; tries to find open patterns.

LT: Blocks first man down to inside for pulling guard.

LG: Pulls right, staying tight to the line of scrimmage. Cuts up through hole and blocks first man through hole.

C: Blocks man over him or immediate linebacker. Makes cut-off block after original contact.

RT: Makes drive block on man over him to set up good double-team block.

TE: Makes double-team block with RT. Makes high block to help seal inside.

QB: Makes reverse pivot, makes pitch to three back. Should have rotation on the ball for a good pitch.

FB: Blocks DE or LB with outside positioning.

RH: Takes two steps forward, then flares hard to the outside to block first man outside.

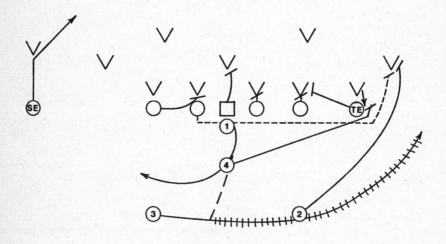

Diagram 3-11

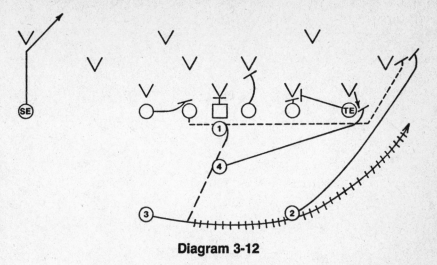

Diagram 3-12

LH: Steps right, runs hard to his right. Looks ball into his hands on pitch from QB. Keeps running hard toward sideline, turns upfield at first opportunity.

Sweep 27 (Diagram 3-13—Even, Diagram 3-14—Odd)

SE: Sprints to inside, picks up first pursuit. Tries to stay under control and, facing his man, blocks him above the waist.

LT: Blocks man over him and makes cut-off block. If defensive man is outside shade, attacks outside leg and uses reverse crab block.

LG: Blocks man over him or immediate LB. Makes cut-off block.

C: Fills for guard on cut-off block or blocks immediate LB.

RG: Pulls left down line of scrimmage, turns upfield, blocks first man.

RT: Blocks man over him and goes downfield.

TE: Hits man over, then releases downfield on down-out pattern.

QB: Reverse pivots, hands off to two back. Fakes keeper and pass to TE.

FB: Drives hard to outside, blocking first loose man. Tries to help seal pursuit.

LH: Drives hard and blocks outside corner or first man to outside.

RH: Steps forward, heads toward 7 hole. Moves ball to left-hand arm and follows blocking.

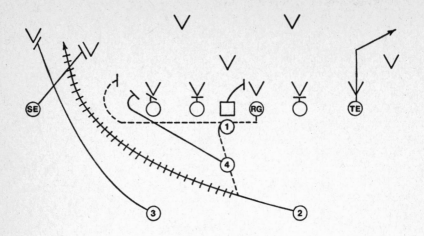

Diagram 3-13

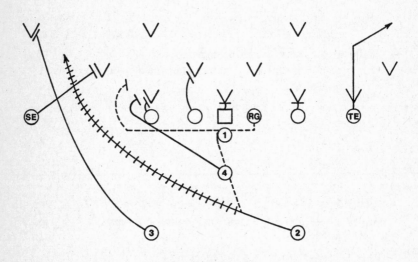

Diagram 3-14

Sweep 29 (Diagram 3-15—Even, Diagram 3-16—Odd)

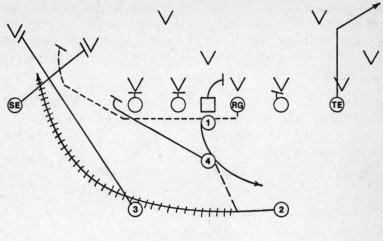

Diagram 3-15

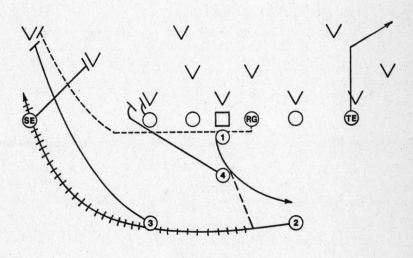

Diagram 3-16

Power 34 (Diagram 3-17)

The 34 power play attacks the 5-2 defenses best. Again, most coaches will play the five-man front against the Pro-Bone because they have seen the 5-2 used against the Wishbone and the Veer. The 34 and 23 are hard plays to stop because offensive people outnumber defensive people on the line of scrimmage, and because of the excellent blocking angle of the fullback.

TE: Blocks man over, forces him outside, releases downfield.

RT: Drive blocks defensive tackle over him back. Uses four-point crab block, drives head under defensive man and drives him off the line of scrimmage.

RG: Seal blocks the middle guard with the center.

C: Crab blocks middle guard, setting double-team.

LG: Blocks immediate linebacker.

LT: Forces defensive man outside and downfield.

SE: Runs short post pattern.

FB: Seal blocks with the RT.

RH: Heads straight through 4 hole, blocks immediate linebacker.

LH: Follows RH through the hole.

QB: Turns and hands off to LH, carries out fake pass to SE.

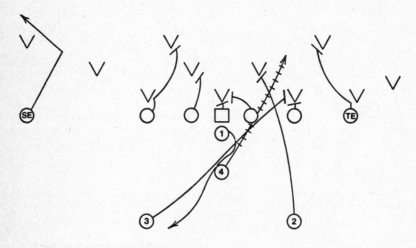

Diagram 3-17

Power 23 (Diagram 3-18)

As seen in Diagram 3-18, Power 23 is the mirror of Power 34. The odd-man front is set up to cover option attacks, and is weaker against a power running game. However, the 4-3 or 6-1 are also vulnerable against the run. In the Pro-Bone, the linemen can be split further (to wide split), which moves defensive linemen out with them. Diagram 3-19 shows the blocking for the Power 34 against the 4-3. Diagram 3-20 shows this blocking for the Power 23.

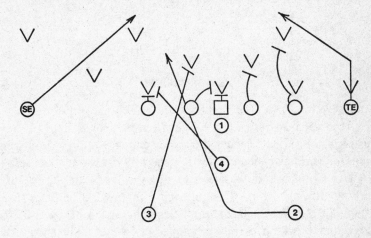

Diagram 3-18

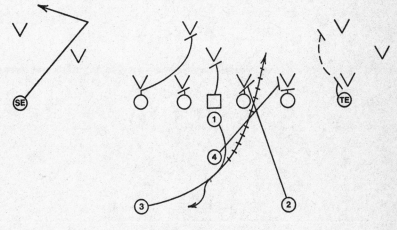

Diagram 3-19

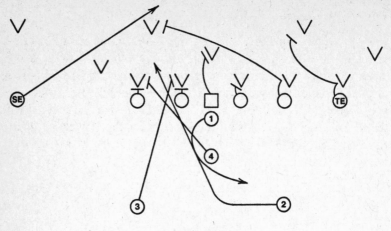

Diagram 3-20

A power lead series can be run from the Power 23-34 series. This series of plays is designed for short yardage on gap or blitzing defenses. The power lead series is generally run from short splits.

The two ways of blocking the power leads are wedge and blocking down to gap. The fullback and on-side halfback lead through the hole for the ball carrier. See Diagrams 3-21 and 3-22 for wedge and blocking down techniques. Diagram 3-21 shows the wedge technique. Diagram 3-22 illustrates blocking down.

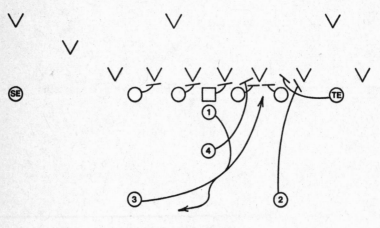

Diagram 3-21

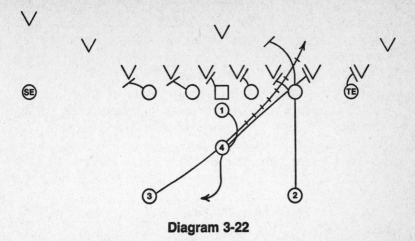

Diagram 3-22

To get even greater blocking power, a coach could use his three best blockers in an unbalanced line (putting the three best blockers together).

The power running offense makes the defense move in en masse to stop the run. This creates one-on-one coverage situations with pass receivers. The passing situation is further enhanced because of the protection in front of the quarterback. The quarterback can fake the handoff on the power series and bootleg pass to the split end or tight end.

The tight end can slip off his block and go straight downfield, giving the quarterback a nice dump pass target. This action also keeps the defensive halfback from coming up hard to stop the power running series.

COUNTERS, CROSSBUCKS AND REVERSES

We come now to the third of our five series of plays, those involving crossbucks, quick pitches, lead options, and reverses. These plays provide counter action to keep defensive flow down. The quick pitches keep defensive ends honest because of the threat of the quick outside attack.

The Pro-Bone gives the offensive halfbacks excellent positioning. Their depth and width make it possible for them to get outside quickly. This must be respected by the defensive ends.

Additionally, the lead option gives the pitch man a blocker in front of him. As mentioned earlier, the fullback's blocking angle gives him good blocking position coming out of the backfield.

Virtually every offense builds counter action into the backfield flow to help cut down defensive pursuit. The Pro-Bone, with the counter action of the fullback, does this from the option set. The crossbucks and reverses complete the cycle of having opposite action for each offensive series. The defense must stay home and not flow with the action of the backs. Running backs consequently have possibilities for greater yardage, and they are less likely to absorb the punishment of gang tackling. The opposite action also minimizes the keys a defense can use.

Reverses are effective, followed by fake reverses with the halfback keeping the ball.

The counter action also makes slant-down defenses less effective because they have too much inside leverage. They must maintain some outside leverage to set for the counter action.

CROSSBUCKS

Crossbuck plays are shown in Diagrams 3-23 through 3-26.

Crossbuck 23 (Diagram 3-23—Even, Diagram 3-24—Odd)

SE: Runs 10-yard sprint pattern, tries to take defensive corner out of play. Can run circle curl for pass off the running play.

LT: Blocks first LB or inverts to the inside of man over him.

LG: Blocks man over or immediate LB. Uses cut-off block to keep his body between ball carrier and defensive man.

C: Blocks man over or immediate LB.

RG: Pulls close to the line of scrimmage, trapping first man outside the guard.

RT: Blocks man over or immediate LB.

TE: Hits man over, then goes downfield for cut-off block, or to block downfield pursuit.

QB: Reverse pivots right, opening up to let guard go by. Makes short fake to FB and continues down the line deep enough to let the trapping guard get by. Continues out to carry out fake pass to SE.

FB: Takes short fake from QB, blocks man in front of pulling guard.

LH: Flares hard to the outside or runs sprint out pattern. Takes pass if corner comes up hard.

RH: Takes four steps left, then cuts into 3 hole behind the trap block of the guard.

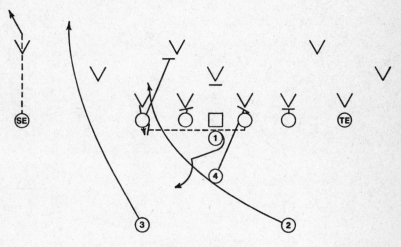

Diagram 3-23

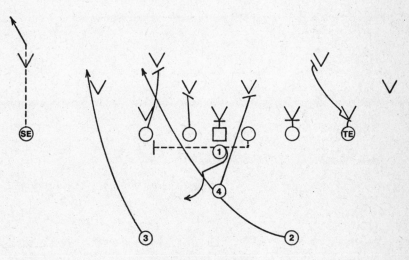

Diagram 3-24

Crossbuck 34 (Diagram 3-25—Even, Diagram 3-26—Odd)

SE: Runs 10-yard sprint post pattern. Should test defense on plays like this. Play action pass can be thrown.

LT: Blocks man over with inside shoulder. Releases to LB.

LG: Pulls close to line of scrimmage, traps first man outside of guard.

C: Blocks man over or immediate LB.

RG: Blocks man over or immediate LB. Uses cut-off block to keep body between ball carrier and defensive man.

RT: Takes inside path if man is over, or goes outside to block first man downfield.

TE: Blocks first LB to the inside.

QB: Makes short fake to the FB and continues reverse pivot, handing off to the three back going through the 4 hole. Does not come down tight to the line—must leave room for the pulling guard. Continues down the line, carrying out fake pass option to the two back.

FB: Takes short fake and blocks man in front of pulling guard.

RH: Flares hard to the outside on sprint out pattern. Can take pass if HB or CB do not cover.

LH: Takes four steps right, then cuts into the 4 hole behind the trap block of the guard.

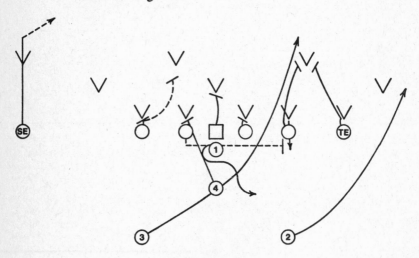

Diagram 3-25

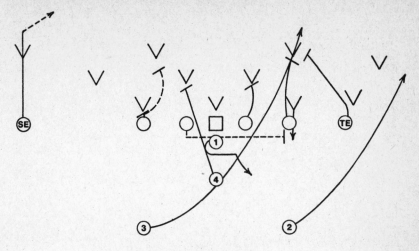

Diagram 3-26

QUICK PITCHES

Quick pitch plays are shown in Diagrams 3-27 through 3-30.

Quick Pitch 28 (Diagram 3-27—Even, Diagram 3-28—Odd)

SE: Runs 10-yard post pattern.

LT: Hits man over outside, goes downfield.

LG: Hits man over or immediate LB.

C : Blocks man over or immediate LB.

RG: Blocks man over or immediate LB.

RT: Pulls hard to outside for lead block for two back.

TE: Blocks man over. Attacks outside leg and makes cut-off block.

QB: Reverse pivots left, pitches to flaring two back. When running fake pitch, extends arms and lets three back take handoff.

FB: Blocks first man to outside. Has taken handoff earlier for key breaker.

RH: Flares hard to outside, watches ball into hands, follows RT's lead block.

LH: Play can be run two ways: QB can call three back flare left for pass or pitch, or Fake Pitch 28-34—a handoff to the three back through the 4 hole.

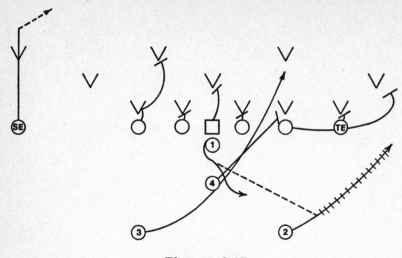

Diagram 3-27

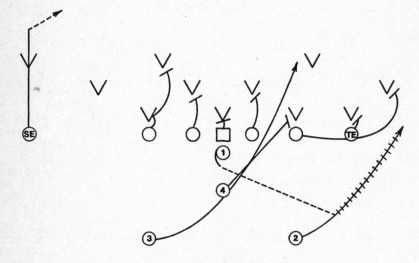

Diagram 3-28

Quick Pitch 37 (Diagram 3-29—Even, Diagram 3-30—Odd)

SE: Starts 10-yard post pattern, stops at 5 yards and blocks DH. Makes cut-off, reverse body block.

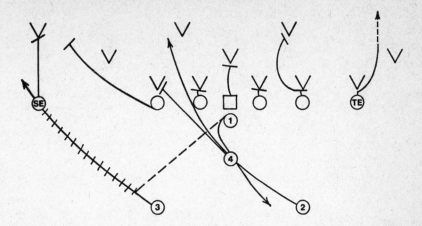

Diagram 3-29

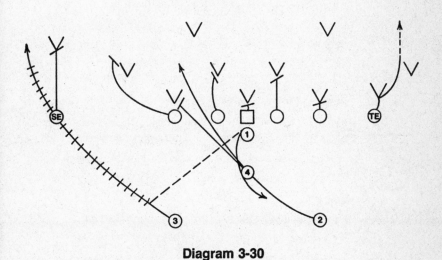

Diagram 3-30

LT: Pulls to outside, makes lead block for three back.

LG: Blocks man over or immediate LB. Makes cut-off, reverse body block.

C: Blocks man over or immediate LB. Makes cut-off, reverse body block.

RG: Blocks man over or immediate LB.

RT: Blocks man over or immediate LB. Makes block, then goes downfield.

TE: Hits man over, then releases downfield for pass.

QB: Reverse pivots right, pitches the ball to flaring three back. When fake pitch is run, extends arms, then hands off to two back. Continues fake or pass to TE.

FB: Blocks first man to outside. Has taken earlier handoff for key breaker.

LH: Flares hard to outside, watches ball into hands, follows LT's lead block.

RH: Play can be run two ways: QB can call two flare left for pass or pitch, or Fake Pitch 37-23—a handoff to the two back through the 3 hole.

LEAD OPTION LEFT AND RIGHT

Lead option plays are shown in Diagrams 3-31 through 3-34.

Lead Option Left (Diagram 3-31—Even, Diagram 3-32—Odd)

SE: Runs 10-yard flag pattern.

LT: Makes drive block on man over or inside. Tries to take man off line of scrimmage, then cut him off with reverse crab block.

LG: Blocks man over or immediate LB. Makes reverse crab block.

C :   Blocks man over or immediate LB. Makes cut-off block.

RG: Blocks man over or immediate LB. Makes cut-off block.

RT: Hits man outside. Releases for downfield blocking.

TE: Hits man over. Releases downfield to block.

QB: Does not reverse pivot. Opens left, goes straight down the line and hands off to the three back, or continues down the line on the option.

FB: Steps left, comes from behind the three back to lead block. Blocks DE if DE comes in hard.

LH: Dives straight ahead, reading the block of the tackle. Carries out fake 8 yards downfield. Action provides good pocket for QB.

RH: Flares outside, looks for pitch from QB.

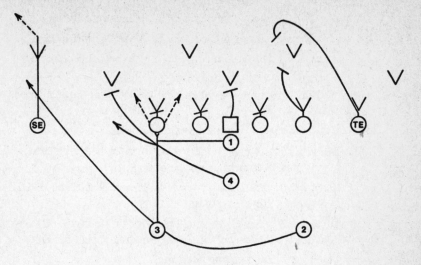

Diagram 3-31

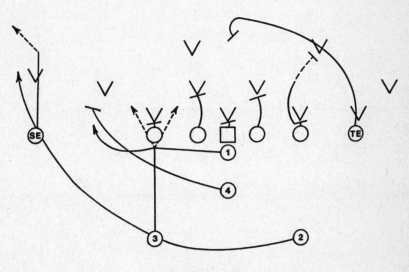

Diagram 3-32

Lead Option Right (Diagram 3-33—Even, Diagram 3-34—Odd)

SE: Runs 10-yard post pattern.

LT: Hits man outside, releases for downfield blocking.

LG: Blocks man over or immediate LB. Makes cut-off block.

C: Blocks man over or immediate LB. Makes cut-off block.

RG: Blocks man over or immediate LB. Makes reverse crab block.

RT: Makes drive block on man over or inside. Tries to drive man off line of scrimmage, then cut him off with reverse crab block.

TE: Hits man over, releases downfield to block.

QB: Does not reverse pivot. Opens straight down the line, hands off to two back or continues on the option.

FB: Steps right, comes from behind two back to lead block. If DE comes hard, FB blocks him.

RH: Dives straight ahead, reading the block of the tackle. Carries fake out 8 yards downfield, provides good pocket for QB.

LH: Flares outside, looks for pitch from QB.

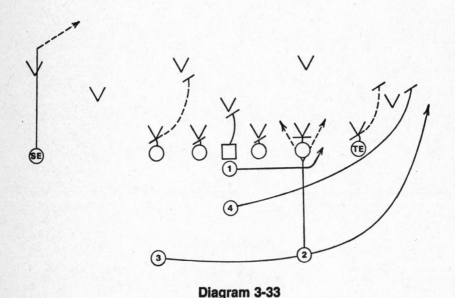

Diagram 3-33

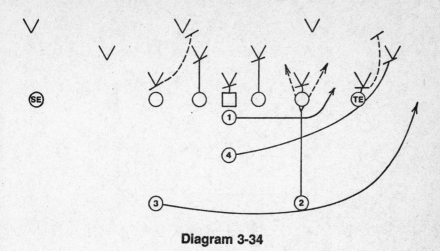

Diagram 3-34

REVERSES

Diagrams 3-35 through 3-38 show the reverse plays mentioned earlier.

325 Reverse (Diagram 3-35—Even, Diagram 3-36—Odd)

Line: Blocks first man to the inside.

TE: Blocks DH.

QB: Reverse pivots, handing off to LH. Continues rollout and blocks DH.

FB: Blocks in space created by pulling guard.

LH: Takes handoff from QB, runs 38 Sweep route. Hands ball off to RH, who is going back to the inside. Continues sweep action fake.

RH: Takes four steps toward DE, then steps on right foot and pivots back to the inside to take handoff from LH. Follows the trap blocking guards through the hole.

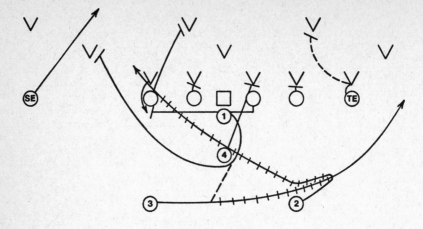

Diagram 3-35

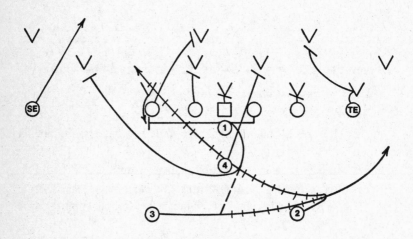

Diagram 3-36

326 Reverse (Diagram 3-37—Even, Diagram 3-38—Odd)

The blocking for the 326 Reverse is a mirror of the 325 Reverse.

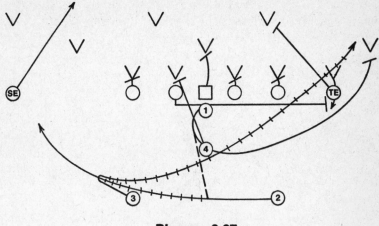

Diagram 3-37

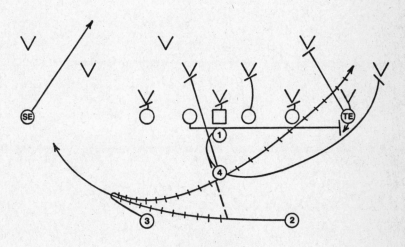

Diagram 3-38

PLAYS USING MOTION

We come now to the fourth group of plays, those using motion. To further utilize the Pro-Wishbone as a passing offense, motion can be used from the halfback or fullback without harm to the running attack. Two more basic plays are shown in Diagram 3-39 (Quick Pitch Regular 28) and Diagram 3-40 (Quick Pitch Trap

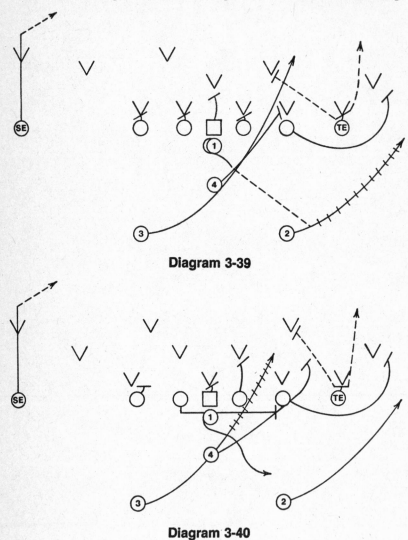

Diagram 3-39

Diagram 3-40

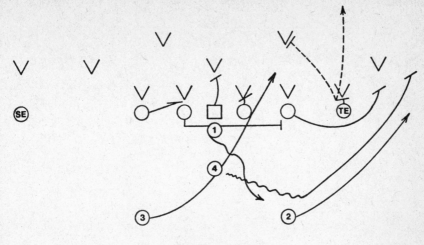

Diagram 3-41

34—Odd). Notice how the blocking is the same, but the defense is given a different look, making them uncertain as to what is going to be run. Diagram 3-41 will show Quick Pitch Right run in yet a third way, the Quick Pitch FB Motion, Trap 34 or Pitch.

Each play has been described with full play action, but you may wish to shorten the play call to suit your own style. You should build your system using your own vocabulary. Plays are more readily identified and learned when this is the case.

Fullback Motion, Quick Pitch 28

Diagrams 3-42 (even) and 3-43 (odd) show the full blocking and backfield action for this play.

SE: Runs 10-yard post pattern.

LT: Blocks man over, or blocks down of defensive man over guard.

LG: Pulls and traps first man outside of offensive guard.

C : Blocks man over or immediate LB.

RG: Blocks man over or immediate LB.

RT: Pulls and makes lead block for two back.

TE: Makes cut-off block on man over, then releases downfield, either to block DH or run pass pattern.

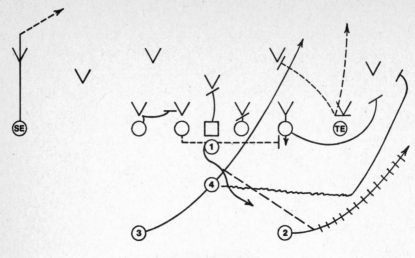

Diagram 3-42

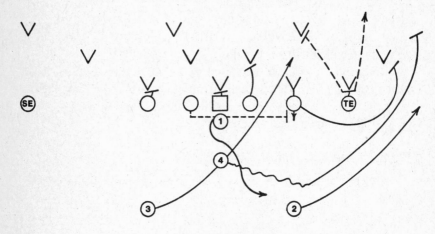

Diagram 3-43

QB: Makes reverse pivot left, pitches ball with spin to two back. Carries out fake handoff to three back, then comes up as if to pass to TE.

FB: Goes in motion just beyond TE, turns upfield and blocks first man to inside.

RH: Flares to outside, receives the ball from QB. Turns upfield, following blocks of FB and pulling RT.

LH: Comes hard toward 4 hole, takes fake handoff from QB, carries out fake upfield.

Sweep 38 (Diagram 3-44)

Let us now look at the Sweep 38 action, shown in Diagrams 3-44 and 3-45, and see how motion can be utilized. Throwing is effective out of motion; the quarterback keeps after fake handoffs and pitches, then throws. Notice that the passes are not long, and motion plays put additional pressure on defensive corners and halfbacks.

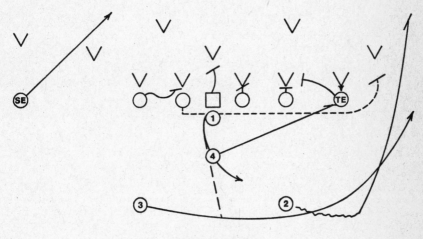

Diagram 3-44

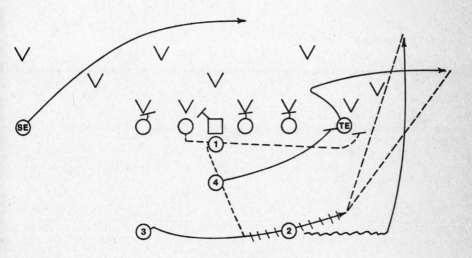

Diagram 3-45

From the Sweep 38 HB Motion shown in Diagram 3-45, the HB pass can be thrown (Diagram 3-46) and the 80 Series, described in Chapter 5, can be utilized. The only changes in blocking are that the guard doesn't go downfield, and the center area blocks over or to the left side. In the 80 Series RH Motion (Diagram 3-47), the changes from the Sweep 38 are that the QB reverse pivots, fakes a

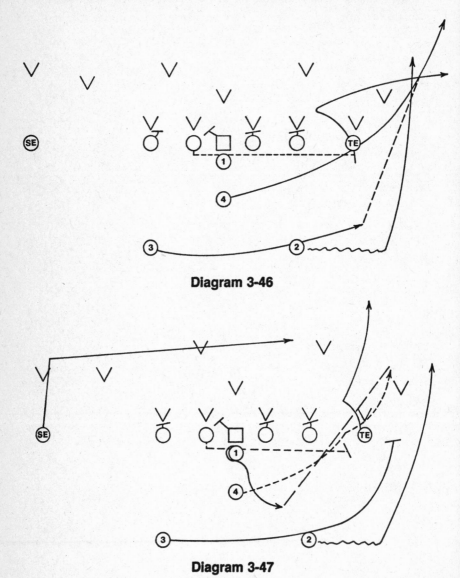

Diagram 3-46

Diagram 3-47

pitch to the three back who is running a sweep, brings the ball back in, and throws to the halfback in motion. If the halfback is covered, the quarterback can take a 7-yard drop and pass to the tight end. The center area blocks over or to the left side. A short pass to the fullback can also be thrown off this play.

SPECIALTY PLAYS

The plays just covered are the basic complements of the Pro-Wishbone option. The option has an excellent chance of succeeding, since the offense has the capacity to generate power, quickness and trapping, all from the same set. Still more offense can be added through small changes, illustrated in the following plays, without changes in the blocking assignments in the line or backfield. These are the specialty plays, the fifth in this chapter's series.

Again, the offense can be adjusted to fit personnel. If a good trapping guard is available, his trap blocking can be emphasized, or the fullback can be used as a trap blocker without changing the offensive formation.

Notice that the blocking assignments in the line are easy to learn and teach. Further versatility in the offense will be seen in Chapter 4, where changes in the line spacing and different cadence counts are described.

The following diagrams illustrate the use of different blocking for the Quick Pitch 28-39, plus the use of a short inside trap to complement the 38 Sweep. With the quarterback using the reverse pivot, this same quarterback action can lead to the crossbuck series, where the quarterback fakes to the fullback and hands to the halfback coming across. Check the assignments for these plays against the regular series, and notice how easily the line blocking is adapted (Diagrams 3-48 through 3-51).

Fake Quick Pitch Trap 23
(Diagram 3-48—Even, Diagram 3-49—Odd)

SE: Blocks first man to inside. Blocks above the waist.

LT: Pulls and makes lead block for three back.

LG: Blocks man over or immediate LB.

C : Blocks man over or immediate LB.

RG: Pulls and traps first man outside of offensive guard.

RT: Blocks man over, or blocks down on defensive man over guard.

TE: Blocks man over, then releases downfield for pass.

QB: Reverse pivots right, fakes pitch to three back, hands off to two back, then comes up as if to pass to TE.

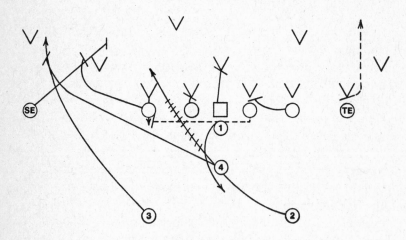

Diagram 3-48

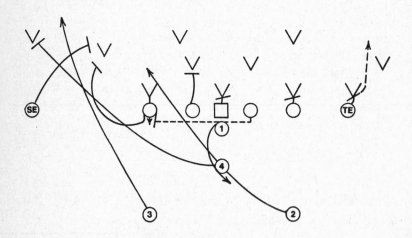

Diagram 3-49

FB: Goes in motion just beyond LT, turns upfield and blocks first man.

RH: Comes hard toward 3 hole, takes handoff from QB, carries upfield.

LH: Flares to outside as if to receive ball from QB, then turns upfield, following the blocks of the FB and the pulling LT.

Fake Quick Pitch 28, Trap 34
(Diagram 3-50—Even, Diagram 3-51—Odd)

SE: Runs 10-yard post pattern.

LT: Blocks man over, or blocks down on defensive man over guard.

LG: Pulls and traps first man outside offensive guard.

C : Blocks man over or immediate LB.

RG: Blocks man over or immediate LB.

RT: Pulls and leads blocking for two back.

TE: Makes cut-off block on man over. Could go to reverse crab block.

QB: Pivots left, makes fake pitch to the two back. Makes handoff to three back, then comes up as if to pass to SE.

FB: Flares outside tackle, turns upfield and blocks first man to inside.

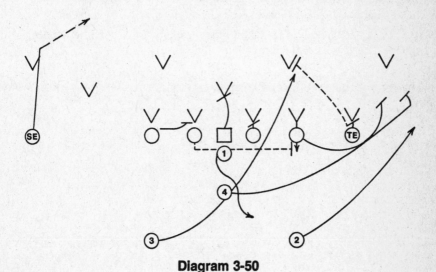

Diagram 3-50

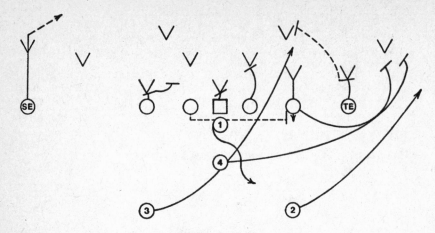

Diagram 3-51

RH: Flares outside, receives fake from QB, then turns upfield, following blocks of FB and pulling RT.

LH: Comes hard toward 4 hole, takes handoff from QB. Carries straight upfield.

These plays demonstrate four advantages of the Pro-Wishbone:

1. Many play sets are available from the original offensive set.
2. There are few changes of blocking or backfield action for each play run from the same basic set.
3. Available personnel are utilized effectively.
4. The defense has a hard time reading what is going to happen.

4

Adding Supplemental Plays
to the Pro-Bone Offenses

In Chapter 3 we made the point that offenses need plays that take advantage of keying defenses. We showed that the Pro-Bone is not easily keyed because the defense is held by the counter action of the fullback away from the motion of the other backs. When the defense must stay home, pursuit is held down and backs find themselves in more one-on-one situations with defensive players.

This chapter introduces additional plays that build on this concept. Being aware that an offense has counter and reverse action, defenses must spend valuable practice time preparing for plays that may never be used. If they don't spend the practice time, they could be caught unprepared. Using special plays just before halftime can cause the coaching staff to spend precious time talking about defense for a limited offense, leaving the regular offense with fewer adjustments to make against the defense in the second half.

With the good running angles provided by the depth and positioning of the running backs, power leads and wedge blocking can be used for entire ball games. The power lead play helps the offense to keep the ball, use up the clock, and put blockers in front of the ball carriers, thus minimizing the danger of fumbling.

The 32 Lead is a power series that can be used in short yardage situations. The blocking for the play affords the quarterback good protection should he decide to fake the handoff and throw to the split end or tight end.

To change the look of the play, the 32 Lead can use wall-off blocking. The latter is effective against an odd-man front. (See Diagram 4-1.) The guard can make a short pull. The quarterback is stepping back to hand off, leaving room for the pulling guard.

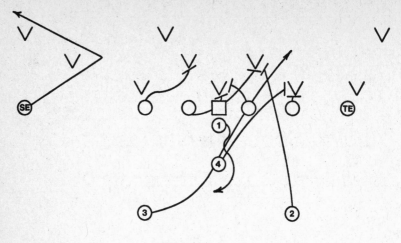

Diagram 4-1

Conventional blocking for the 32 Lead against both even and odd fronts is shown in Diagrams 4-2 and 4-3. Diagrams 4-4 through 4-7 show the blocking of the 34 and 23 Leads against a gap defense.

32 Lead (Diagram 4-2—Even, Diagram 4-3—Odd)

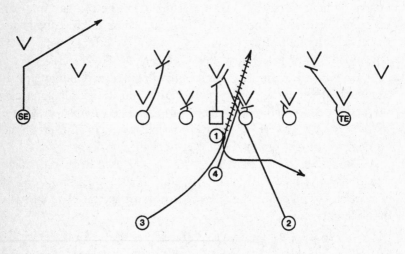

Diagram 4-2

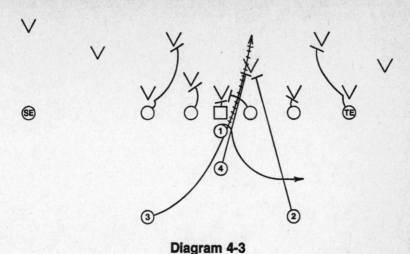

Diagram 4-3

SE: Runs 10-yard post pattern.

LT: Blocks through man. Goes downfield and blocks first man.

LG: Blocks man over or immediate LB. Makes cut-off block.

C: Blocks man over or immediate LB. If man over, makes double-team block with guard by outside leg charge.

RG: Makes double-team block on man over with RB, attacks outside leg. If no man over, makes double-team block with center.

RT: Blocks man over or immediate LB. Makes cut-off block.

TE: Hits man over. Makes outside release and goes downfield for block or pass.

FB: Blocks first man through hole.

QB: Hands off to three back. Reverses and fakes throw to TE.

RH: Goes through 3 hole, blocks first man.

LH: Takes handoff, follows two back through 2 hole.

34 Lead Gap Defense (Diagram 4-4)

SE: Runs 10-yard post pattern.

LT: Blocks first man outside left.

LG: Blocks first man outside left.

C : Blocks first man outside left.

RG: Blocks first man to the left.

RT: Blocks first man to the right.

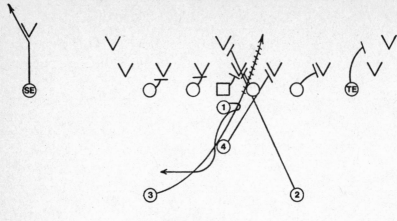

Diagram 4-4

TE: Blocks first man to the outside, then releases for pass.
QB: Hands off to three back, carries out fake pass.
RH: Makes lead block through 4 hole, blocks first man.
LH: Takes handoff, follows blocking through 4 hole.

23 Lead Odd Gap Defense (Diagram 4-5)

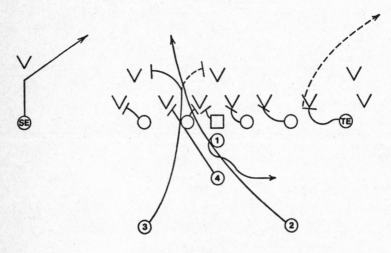

Diagram 4-5

SE: Runs 10-yard post pattern.

LT: Blocks first man to the left.

LG: Blocks first man to the right.

C: Blocks linebacker.

RG: Blocks first man to the left.

RT: Blocks first man to the left.

TE: Blocks first man to the left, then releases for pass.

QB: Hands off to two back and carries out fake pass.

FB: Blocks first loose man to the left.

LH: Makes lead block.

RH: Takes handoff, follows blocking through 3 hole.

23 Lead (Diagram 4-6—Even, Diagram 4-7—Odd)

SE: Runs 10-yard post flag pattern.

LT: Blocks first man to inside or immediate linebacker. Makes drive block outside, then reverse crab block for cut-off.

LG: Pulls and blocks first man to the outside. Drive blocks the outside defensive leg down the line of scrimmage.

C: Blocks man over or immediate linebacker. Makes cut-off block.

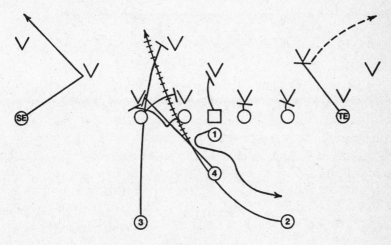

Diagram 4-6

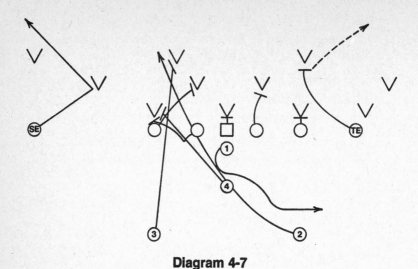

Diagram 4-7

RG: Blocks man over or immediate linebacker. Makes cut-off
   block.

RT: Blocks man over or immediate LB. Makes cut-off block.

TE: Releases downfield, makes block on DH. Should be ready to
   receive pass.

QB: Makes open-hand handoff to RH. Reverses and fakes throw to
   TE.

FB: Makes double-team block with guard on first man outside.

LH: Goes through 3 hole, blocks DH.

RH: Takes handoff, follows blocking through 3 hole.

   The trap series helps to make the option plays more effective.
The defensive tackle will have been "softened up" by the aggressive, one-on-one blocking of the offensive tackle. The latter should
use inside shoulder technique and release to the linebacker.

   The quarterback must lose ground coming down the line of
scrimmage to make room for the pulling guard.

   The quarterback, in making his reverse pivot, opens up more
with his left foot when turning, thus permitting the extra distance
from the line of scrimmage. Diagrams 4-8 through 4-11 show Traps
34 and 23.

Trap 34 (Diagram 4-8—Even, Diagram 4-9—Odd)

SE: Runs 10-yard sprint post pattern. Should test defense. Can receive play action pass off this play.

LT: Blocks man over or immediate LB.

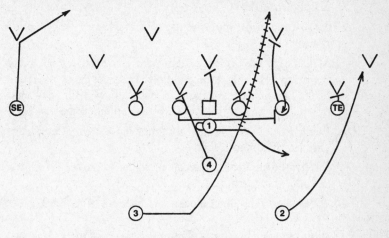

Diagram 4-8

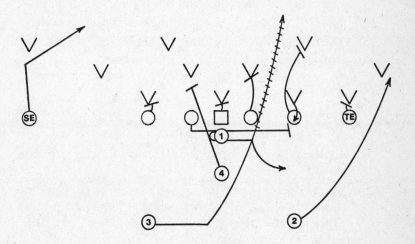

Diagram 4-9

LG: Pulls close to line of scrimmage, traps first man outside guard.

C : Blocks man over or immediate LB.

RG: Blocks man over or immediate LB. Uses cut-off block, keeps his body between ball carrier and defensive man.

RT: Takes inside path if man is over, or goes outside to block first man downfield.

TE: Makes hard drive block on man over, goes to reverse cut-off block.

QB: Makes short fake to FB, continues reverse reverse pivot, handing off to LH going through 4 hole. Does not come down tight to the line; must leave room for the pulling guard. Continues down the line, carrying out fake pass option to the two back.

RH: Flares hard to the outside on sprint out pattern. Can receive pass if DBs do not cover.

LH: Takes four steps right, then cuts into the 4 hole behind the trap block of the guard.

FB: Takes short fake, then blocks man in front of pulling guard.

Trap 23 (Diagram 4-10—Even, Diagram 4-11—Odd)

SE: Runs 10-yard sprint flag pattern to run off defensive corner. Can run circle curl for pass off running play.

LT: Blocks first LB or invert to the inside of immediate man.

LG: Blocks man over or immediate LB. Uses cut-off block to keep body between ball carrier and defensive man.

C : Blocks man over or immediate LB.

RG: Pulls close to line of scrimmage. Traps first man outside the guard.

RT: Blocks man over or immediate LB.

TE: Hits man over. Goes downfield for cut-off block on downfield pursuit.

QB: Makes reverse pivot right, opening up to let guard go by. Makes short fake to FB, then continues down the line deep enough for the trapping guard to get by. Hands off to RH. Carries out fake pass to SE.

FB: Takes short fake and blocks man in front of pulling guard.

LH: Flares hard to the outside on sprint out pattern. Can take pass if CB comes up hard.

RH: Takes four steps left, then cuts into the 3 hole behind the block of the trapping guard.

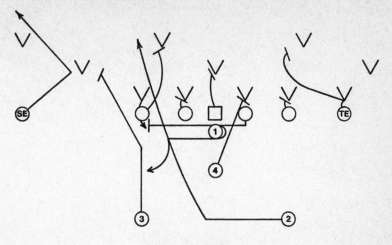

Diagram 4-10

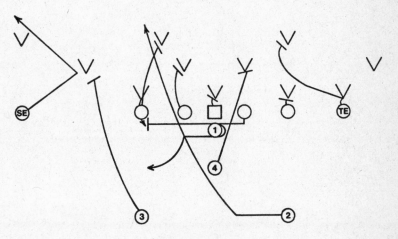

Diagram 4-11

The Quick Pitch 37 Fullback Trap 23 helps to keep the defensive tackle from tailgating if the latter is reading the offensive tackle. This play takes advantage of the fullback's blocking angle. It is especially effective against a gapped defense, because the fullback blocks the first man to the outside, creating an especially good running lane for the halfback. See Diagram 4-12 for gap blocking.

Diagrams 4-13 and 4-14 show this play against conventional even (4-13) and odd (4-14) fronts.

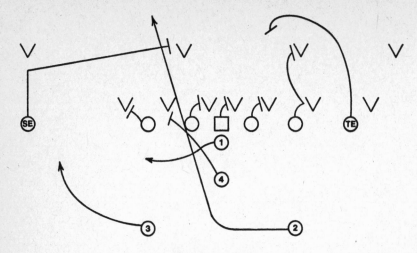

Diagram 4-12

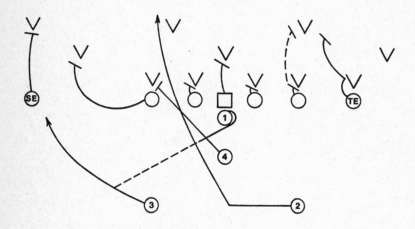

Diagram 4-13

Quick Pitch 37 Fullback Trap 23

SE: Starts 10-yard post pattern, stops at 5 yards and blocks DH. Makes cut-off, reverse body block.

LT: Pulls to outside, makes lead block for three back.

LG: Blocks man over or immediate LB. Makes cut-off, reverse body block.

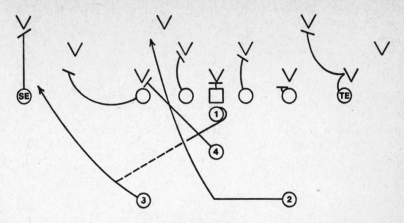

Diagram 4-14

C: Blocks man over or immediate LB. Makes cut-off, reverse body block.

RG: Blocks man over or immediate LB.

RT: Blocks man over or immediate LB. Hits man, then goes downfield.

TE: Hits man over, then releases downfield for pass.

QB: Makes reverse pivot right, pitches ball to flaring LH. When running fake quick pitch, extends arms and hands off to RH. Continues fake or passes to TE.

LH: Flares hard, watches pitch into his arms, follows lead block of LT.

RH: Play can be run two ways: QB can call either RH flare left for pass or pitch, or fake pitch 37-23—a handoff to the RH through the 3 hole.

FB: Blocks first man to the outside. Will have taken handoff earlier for key breaker.

QB Power Rollout

The Power Rollouts by the quarterback are good plays if you have a strong runner at the position. This set offers him excellent protection on the rollout pass and good outside positioning for the run. From this set, halfback draws can be incorporated, thus cutting down the defensive flow. See Diagrams 4-15 (even), 4-16 (odd), and 4-17 (left).

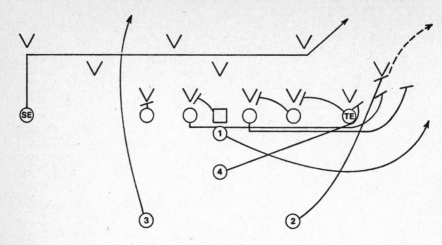

Diagram 4-15

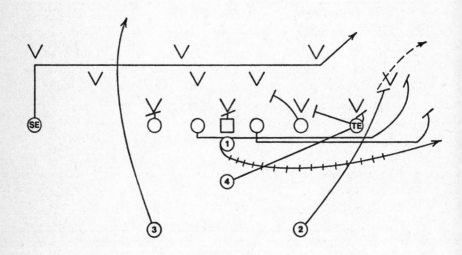

Diagram 4-16

SE: Runs 5-yard sprint, then cuts parallel to line of scrimmage for 15 yards and heads for flag.

RT: Makes drive block on first man inside, goes to crab cut-off block.

RG: Pulls and attacks legs of first defensive man outside.

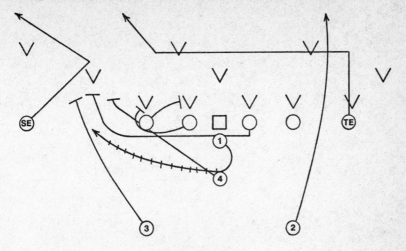

Diagram 4-17

C: Makes drive block on man over or first man to inside gap.
      Goes to cut cut-off block.

LG: Pulls and cuts upfield at first opening. Attacks first man up-
      field.

LT: Makes drive block on man over. Stays with the block, keeps
      the man from inside pursuit.

TE: Makes drive block on first man inside. Goes to crab cut-off
      block.

QB: Sprints outside looking for opening. Checks for open receiv-
      ers, then either runs or passes.

Blocking for the Quarterback Rollout Left is a mirror of the
same play to the right. The assignments for the left tackle, center,
right tackle and tight end are the same. The split end runs a post,
flag pattern.

Tackle Trap

The Tackle Trap is set up by the quarterback rollouts and 36-38
Sweeps. Most teams will key the guards for trapping action. The
Tackle Trap is excellent for counter motion to break defensive keys.
See Diagrams 4-18 (even) and 4-19 (Tackle Trap 13 odd).

The left tackle, left guard, center and right guard all block to
the inside gaps or block the immediate man inside. The fullback and

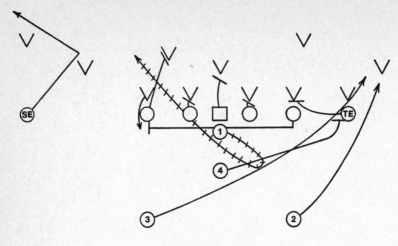

Diagram 4-18

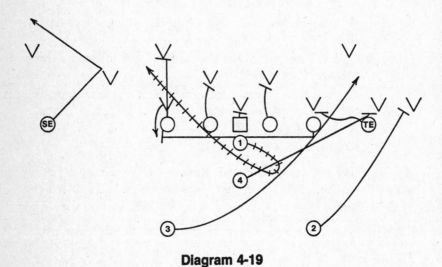

Diagram 4-19

tight end block 36 Sweep action. The right tackle pulls and blocks the first man outside the left guard. The halfbacks run 36 Sweep action. The quarterback starts 36 Sweep action with a reverse pivot for three steps. He then cuts back and runs behind the trapping tackle.

Notice that the blocking techniques for the traps and reverses resemble those for the regular offense. This makes it much more difficult to look for keys. With the material supplied by this chapter, you now have the complete offense—option, power leads, sweeps, and traps—and they all originate from the same set. Simplified blocking is used throughout.

With this system, you can organize drill time to concentrate on blocking techniques, perfecting their use in specific plays. Because each block can be used for different plays, specialized blocking techniques for separate groups of plays need not be taught.

5

Developing the Pro-Bone Passing Attack

Coaches want their passing offense to blend with their running offense. The desirable offense is one in which a formation change is not required to go from one to the other. Running and passing from the same set presents formidable problems for defenses, especially if the formation allows the offense to get deep and outside quickly.

The Pro-Bone is superior to the conventional Wishbone in its incorporation of a dropback passing attack. The Wishbone, in most cases, utilizes different sets or sets a halfback as a flanker, consequently diluting the threat of the run.

Again we return to the question of the available personnel, especially for the quarterback position. The college coach can recruit for a specific need, but the high school coach must make do with the players at hand. The Pro-Bone partly alleviates this problem: It provides ball control, plus wide-open passing, without requiring an outstanding quarterback.

Here are the specific advantages of the Pro-Bone, in terms of providing a balanced passing attack:

1. The Pro-Bone, with the halfbacks 4½ yards deep and aligned with the tackles, gives the halfbacks quick outside release with good sideline depth. The depth of the halfbacks, plus the presence of the split end, causes the defense to spread out, creating better running lanes.

2. The Pro-Bone provides options for rollout (Diagram 5-1), dropback (Diagram 5-2) and play action (Diagram 5-3) from the same set.

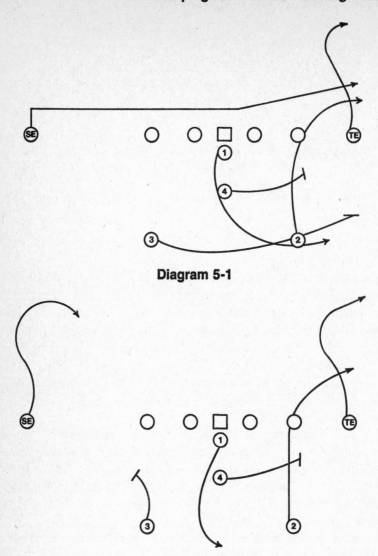

Diagram 5-1

Diagram 5-2

REGULAR PRO-BONE OPTION PASS OFFENSE

Most of the literature on Wishbone throwing suggests that the basic option is enough of a threat to all of the short zones. The Pro-Bone threatens the defense more, essentially because the de-

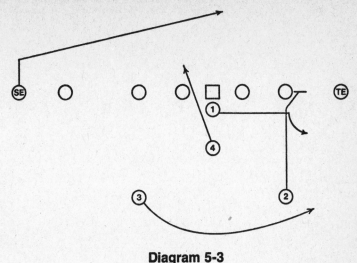

Diagram 5-3

fense must spread out more. This not only creates more one-on-one situations, but it also keeps defensive backs off the line of scrimmage. They are held to their positions by the deep positioning of the halfbacks and the close positioning of the fullback. The fullback, of course, has the potential of a quick thrust up the middle, freezing the middle linebacker and keeping him from dropping into the middle zone quickly to aid the backs. In addition, cornerbacks have to respect the quickness of the halfbacks to the outside, preventing them from achieving deep coverage of the field quickly. This also puts the defender closer to the receiver, making breakaways more likely.

Receivers should be taught the basic pattern tree: look-in, bench, hook inside/outside, flag post, hook and go, hook sideline, Z pattern bench and sideline, sprint out. See Diagram 5-4.

Receivers should not slow down or stop when making their faking steps. This gives the defender time to adjust and to attain better position.

These split-second delays should be reduced as much as possible. A method that helps is coaching the short waggle pattern, which is run from a short S pattern. An exception to this is the quick 50 series, in which the quarterback simply stands straight up and throws. The waggle pattern keeps the defender in constant backward motion. If he gets too close, the receiver cuts off from him and

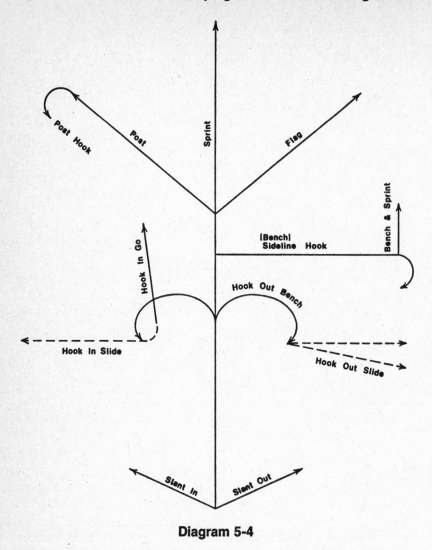

Diagram 5-4

achieves better position to catch the pass. The waggle pattern is discussed more fully later in this chapter, in the section on the 90 series of passing plays.

The option pass offense has a twofold benefit. (Option pass plays are shown in Diagrams 5-6, 5-7 and 5-8.) First, the pass action is from play action, which makes the defensive halfback honor the pass, yet keeps him from coming up hard to stop the running game. Second, pass patterns can be kept short, helping out the quarterback if he has not been blessed with a strong throwing arm.

Option passes do keep the defense loose for the running game. They also keep defenses in a four-deep situation, eliminating some defenses altogether. This helps the offensive preparation each week.

For example, the 5-2 invert would be very difficult to run against the Pro-Bone because of the pass threat and the ease with which the fullback can get to the outside. (See Diagram 5-5.) Running against the four-deep makes the ground game easier to block and run. The defense can be outmanned in blocking a given running area.

The following are the basic Pro-Bone option passing plays.

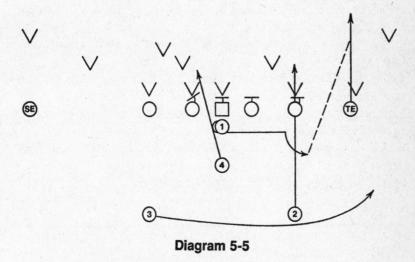

Diagram 5-5

Option Pass Right (Diagram 5-6)

SE: Looks in and runs hard off the line, splitting the CB and HB. The SE is the #3 receiver.

TE: Takes two steps to the inside and sprints out. Watches for ball over left shoulder. TE is primary receiver.

RH: Flares deep outside toward sideline. Watches inside for chest-high pass. He is #2 receiver.

FB: Runs hard to gap, checks for blitz, and knocks down any defensive players in gap.

LH: Runs hard as in the option, veers to the outside and tries to bring HB or CB up.

Line: Blocks (aggressively) defensive men over or inside seam.

QB: Gives good fake to FB who is coming down the line hard.

Reverse pivots, moves down line, puts ball out toward LH, draws ball back in, then lofts it high for TE to run under. If CB comes up, throws to RH.

Coaching point: Teach the QB to loft the ball so that the point comes down for the TE. Before the QB throws, he should bring the ball back to the body after the short fake to the LH, then slide his hand back down the laces and release the ball with a good follow-through afterward. The QB should fake away from the line of scrimmage when throwing.

Note: Within each of the series to be described, individual receivers can alter their routes in response to defensive adjustments.

The option pass is effective when the defense is thinking "run." It is effective on first down and on third down, short yardage.

The option pass simply keeps the defense honest. Patterns should be kept short. Receivers shouldn't look for the ball until they are ready to catch it. This can be accomplished through careful timing of patterns.

Ends can fake blocks on defenders and then break into their patterns. After the end has blocked the defensive halfback on the pitch several times, the option pass opens up.

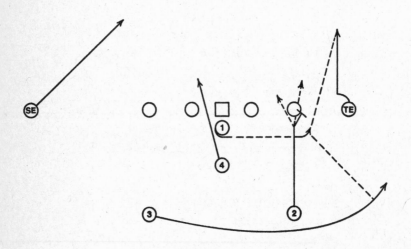

Diagram 5-6

Option Pass Left (Diagram 5-7)

SE: Looks in six steps and Z's out. Goes hard toward LB and cuts off from him at a 90° angle. SE is the primary receiver.

TE: Steps to inside of defensive man, cutting him off. Runs sprint pattern.

LH: Runs deep flare outside. Tries to draw CB up.

RH: Runs regular option, flaring outside of OT and blocking anyone coming up. Carries out good fake.

FB: Runs hard through gap, blocking anyone in gap.

Line: RG moves man toward outside shoulder. Rest of linemen block men over or inside gaps.

QB: Makes good fake to FB, reverse pivots, puts the ball out toward RH, draws it back in, slides fingers down laces, throws loft pass to SE, and flares away from line of scrimmage.

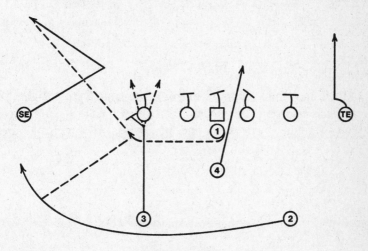

Diagram 5-7

Lead Option Pass Right (Diagram 5-8)

Line: Blocks aggressively off the ball. To reverse crab, cut-off block.

FB: Makes lead block, taking first man to the outside.

LH: Flares as in regular option, but cuts back after six steps for blind-side blocking.

RH: Runs straight dive. Flares to outside flat 6 yards deep.

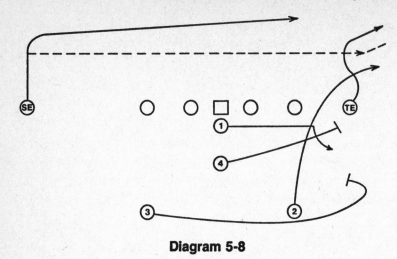

Diagram 5-8

QB: Does not reverse pivot. Opens up straight down line of scrimmage, fakes to RH, flares to the outside looking for the open man.

Lead Option Pass Left (Diagram 5-9)

The Lead Option Left is a mirror of the Lead Option Right. The tight end does come down the line of scrimmage 4 yards deep, clears the middle linebackers, and then breaks for the cleared area.

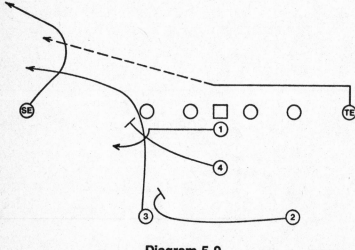

Diagram 5-9

PLAY ACTION PASS PLAYS

Play action passes are more "keep the defense honest" plays. Defensive halfbacks cannot come up hard when they know that the offense will throw from quick outside action or sweeps.

This type of passing does not require inordinate skill. Time can be spent after practice working on halfbacks' passing skills. Halfbacks can also work on their passing during the off season.

The halfbacks should be taught to pass the same as a rollout quarterback: Plant the forward foot and rotate the hips and arms through. Most of the patterns are short, and the near man is usually open.

Quick Pitch Pass Left (Diagram 5-10)

The quick pitch pass keeps the CB honest. He cannot come up hard when the HB flares because of this pass. This pass is not hard to throw and the pattern opens up quickly.

SE: Runs 12-yard flag pattern. Comes off hard four steps inside, then runs flag.

TE: Runs 10-yard banana across safety zone.

FB: QB fakes handoff. FB runs outside hip of LG 5 yards deep into flat.

RH: Flares left and bellies back to block weak side.

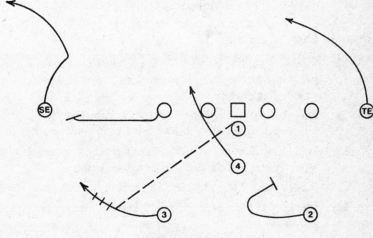

Diagram 5-10

LH: Starts left as in sweep and takes pitch from QB. Looks for open receiver.

QB: Opens up with left foot outside, extends arms for FB to come over for good fake. Pitches ball to LH. The QB's right hand supplies the power for the pitch, with the left hand guiding. After the fake to the FB and the pitch, the QB should come straight back to fake possible deep dropback passing pattern.

Quick Pitch Pass Right (Diagram 5-11)

The Quick Pitch Pass Right is a mirror of the Quick Pitch Pass Left, except that the QB pitches with the left hand and guides with the right.

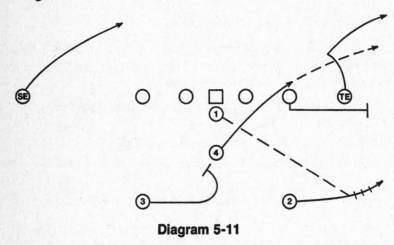

Diagram 5-11

Sweep 36 Pass (Diagram 5-12)

SE: Runs 12-yard flag pattern. Comes off the ball at three-quarters speed and off the cut full speed. This pattern can be run as a waggle flag pattern.

LT: Fills the gap to the inside so that no defensive lineman can follow pulling guard. Blocks LB if LB tries to come through.

LG: Pulls down line of scrimmage, sealing off any penetration or blocking the first defensive man to the outside.

C: Blocks area off left shoulder. Makes sure open area is covered.

RG: Blocks man over or inside seam. Uses inside, should reverse cut-off block.

RT: Blocks inside gap should penetration start to occur. Otherwise, blocks man over seam.

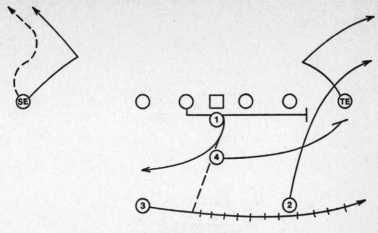

Diagram 5-12

TE: Comes down the line three steps to the inside, as in the start of the double-team, then breaks hard on a rainbow pattern 14 yards deep.

FB: Seals first man to the outside of the offensive tackle.

RH: Sprints straight ahead as if to block the LB, then breaks toward the sideline 6 yards deep.

QB: Reverse pivots, pitches ball to LH, and continues out to fake pass to SE.

LH: Runs regular Sweep 36 route, running hard, making sweep key work for defense. Play is run as option; if receivers are covered, LH runs.

Sweep 27 Pass (Diagram 5-13)

The Sweep 27 Pass is a mirror of the Sweep 36 Pass.

RT: Blocks man over him or inside seam.

RG: Pulls, sealing any penetration or blocking the first man to the outside.

C: Seals right shoulder gap or blocks man over him.

LG: Seals inside gap or blocks man over him.

LT: Blocks inside gap or man over him.

SE: Runs 14-yard deep V pattern, running the first seven steps as a look-in, then breaking to the outside.

LH: Sprints straight ahead as if to block the linebacker, then breaks out in the flat 6 yards deep.

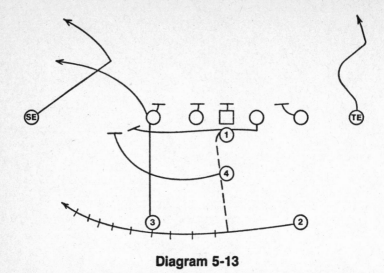

Diagram 5-13

FB: Seals the first man to the outside off the offensive tackle.

QB: Reverse pivots, pitches ball to RH, and continues out to fake pass to TE.

TE: Runs 12-yard flag pattern or waggle outside pattern. Comes off the ball hard.

RH: Runs deep 27 Sweep pattern. Runs hard—option to run if receivers covered.

Stand Up Pass or Stand Up and Go (Diagram 5-14)

The Stand Up Series is to be used when these situations exist: 1) defensive halfbacks are playing deep off the line of scrimmage; 2) you have a quick split end; 3) a blitz forces you to get the ball outside quickly; and 4) a mismatch exists between an offensive and defensive player.

If you have a good runner and receiver, this series of plays can become primary. The defense must 1½-man or 2-man zone this area, thus losing their numerical superiority on the field.

Line: Fires out, blocking to keep defensive men's hands down.

LT: Pulls and lead blocks for SE.

SE: Comes off the line hard two steps, then retreats five steps to receive the ball. In Stand Up and Go, SE comes straight back to draw up CB, then sprints downfield.

TE: Runs sprint out pattern.

LH: Flares to the outside.

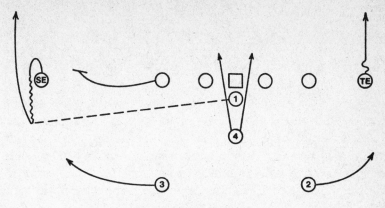

Diagram 5-14

RH: Flares to the outside.

FB: Delays one count, then comes up over the 1 hole.

QB: The play can be run in five different ways.

    1) The QB stands straight up and throws to the SE.

    2) QB runs the FB through the 1 hole, faking to the FB first, then throwing to the SE.

    3) QB stands straight up, fakes the pass to the SE, delays the FB one count, and then turns and hands off to the FB.

    4) QB stands up, fakes throw to SE using pumping action, fakes to the FB, and then passes to either flaring HB.

    5) QB fakes throw to SE, turns around and hits TE.

In yet another variation, the QB can pump once, faking to the SE, allowing the CB to come up, and then let the SE sprint downfield. The QB should lay the ball up in the air and let the SE run under it.

THE 90 SERIES

The 90 series of plays could be the most essential feature of the Pro-Bone as a truly balanced offense. The majority of offenses do not have the dropback passing game off the running set: In the Wishbone, passing is based on the running threat of each play; in the I, because the fullback and tailback are lined up behind the quarterback, possibilities of the backs getting outside quickly are eliminated; in the Pro-Set, the pure passing game is present without the middle threat of the fullback. To defense the Pro-Set, the inside linebackers can drop back more confidently because of the reduced possibility of the run. To reemphasize the complete passing game aspect of the Pro-Bone, it incorporates possibilities to drop back or to use play action, flanker sets, and motion off the same set used for the run.

The 90 series of plays is the dropback series of the passing game. Before describing the plays of the 90 series, pass patterns and timing should be reemphasized and amplified. A major problem can arise in getting receivers to cut and run at full speed in order to get to the reception area at the appropriate time. Timing is critically important. Teams with high percentage rates of completion attain them through timing.

If the waggle pattern is used, the receiver can run a route under control, without stopping or letting the defensive man gain better position. The Pro-Bone does incorporate a cut pattern, but the waggle provides variety. It also provides a teaching opportunity to improve players.

In teaching the waggle pattern, players should be shown both the inside and the outside waggle. Diagram 5-15 illustrates the theory.

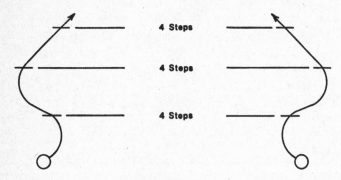

Diagram 5-15

The receiver comes off the line hard to the inside four steps and starts a circle to the inside. The routes are circles. Designating the number of steps should not give receivers the idea that they run in straight lines to particular points—the steps merely indicate distance. From any four-step interval, the receiver can break to any one of the patterns of the pattern tree, such as bench, look-in, or flag. Running the outside waggle, the receiver comes off the line hard to

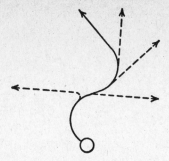

Diagram 5-16

the outside, using the four-step theory. Diagram 5-16 shows how the player can cut off the pattern after the radius of the circle is reached, without losing speed.

This is probably a better way to get open and catch the football. Receivers should be timed for pattern and area. They should be timed from the time the ball is snapped until it reaches the reception area.

As we mentioned earlier, receivers should be taught to count "one-thousand-one, one-thousand-two," and so on, so that they concentrate on the running of the pattern, looking for the ball only when it is due. They should go for the ball at the appropriate time, looking it into their hands. If the receiver looks for the ball before it's thrown, he will not be in his designated area at the appropriate time.

In the 90 series, the flare back is the check-off man in case the quarterback gets into trouble. If the defense employs zones frequently, the 4-4-4 can be changed to 5-5-5 or 3-3-3, to split the zone. Because of the continuous motion employed in this series, the defensive backs must cover loosely, making it easier for receivers to cut off from them to receive the ball. Diagrams 5-17 through 5-22 present the 90 waggle series passing plays.

Pattern 90 (Diagram 5-17)

Linemen come across and make good contact. Then they retreat, forming a pocket. If the line reads blitz they should block to their left. If the defense gaps, the fullback blocks the first man to the outside. The line can also block right and the fullback left. Diagram 5-18 shows the left shoulder gap block.

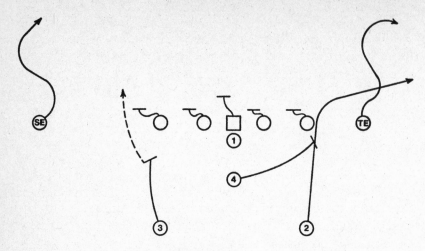

Diagram 5-17

Gap Block 90 (Diagram 5-18)

SE: Runs inside, 12-yard waggle pattern.

LH: Blocks outside man and releases to vacated LB position.

FB: Blocks first man outside of tackle, or picks up first man who stunts.

RH: Sprints toward LB or end. Runs waggle pattern in and bench 5 yards deep.

TE: Runs inside waggle 15 yards deep. Comes back 2 yards.

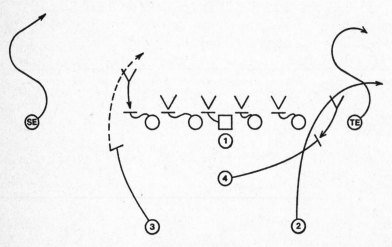

Diagram 5-18

QB: Sprints back nine steps, watches SE, throws to TE. If TE is covered or the rush is hard, looks for halfbacks.

Pattern 91 (Diagram 5-19)

SE: Runs outside waggle 12 yards. Hooks sideline and comes back toward the ball 2 yards.

LH: Blocks outside man and releases to vacated LB position.

FB: Blocks first man outside of tackle, or picks up first man who stunts.

RH: Sprints toward outside linebacker and flag.

TE: Runs inside, 12-yard post pattern.

QB: Sprints back nine steps, watches TE, steps up and throws to RH (primary receiver) or SE.

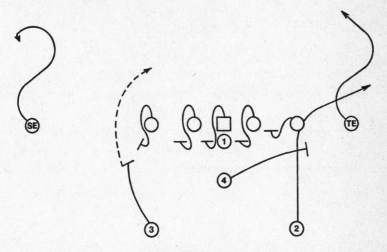

Diagram 5-19

Pattern 92 (Diagram 5-20)

SE: Runs outside waggle, 18-yard flag pattern.

LH: Sprints toward LB, runs 45° bench pattern 8 yards deep.

FB: Blocks first man to the left or picks up any stunt man coming through.

RH: Blocks first man to the outside of tackle. If there is no pressure, he releases to the outside.

TE: Runs inside waggle, 12-yard hook inside.

QB: Sprints back nine steps. Watches TE, pumps once, turns and throws to SE.

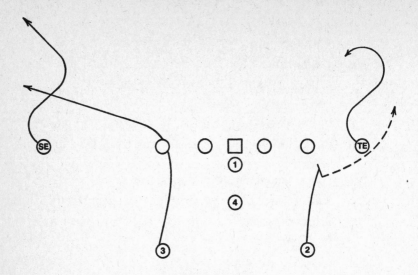

Diagram 5-20

Pattern 93 (Diagram 5-21)

SE: Runs inside waggle post pattern.

LH: Blocks first man to the outside.

FB: Blocks first man outside tackle and sprints out to area cleared by TE and RH. Looks for soft pass.

RH: Sprints to outside and heads upfield, taking CB with him.

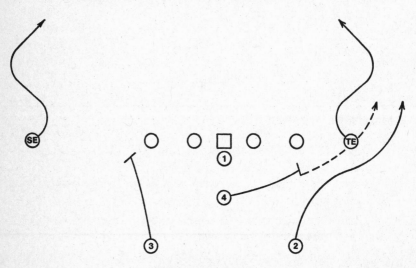

Diagram 5-21

TE: Runs inside waggle, 12-yard post pattern.

QB: Watches TE and SE. If the area clears, he turns and lofts soft pass to FB.

Any of these patterns can be changed. Individual routes can be altered to take advantage of any defensive weakness that may be discovered. For example, Diagram 5-22 is Pattern 91, SE Out Hook and Slide.

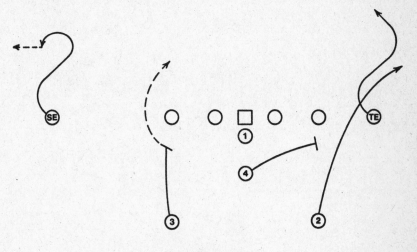

Diagram 5-22

THE 50 QUICK SERIES

The 50 series is the quick passing game. This series can be used when the defense blitzes on certain downs, or when the defense uses uneven coverage. Audibles can be called at the line of scrimmage. The series is good for quick yardage, especially when the defense is playing loose. The 50 series uses aggressive line blocking. Linemen should try to knock defensive people down.

The 50 series can be used effectively from the fake dive or lead option. The closeness of the fullback gives the quarterback the good quick fake. In addition, the linebackers must honor the fullback coming at them. With the linebackers unable to read the pass quickly, the seams in zone coverage should be more open.

The seams close to the line of scrimmage can be hit quickly and effectively from the 50 series. Again, the outside space of the halfbacks makes them quick threats on short outside patterns such as 50-54. Halfbacks can be hit from a double fake. Diagram 5-23, which depicts the 52 Quick Slant, shows how, since the fullback is so close, timing can be accomplished to carry out the double fake.

Diagrams 5-24 through 5-31 give the rest of the plays of the 50 quick series.

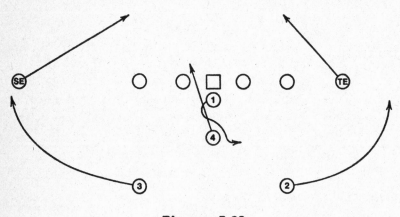

Diagram 5-23

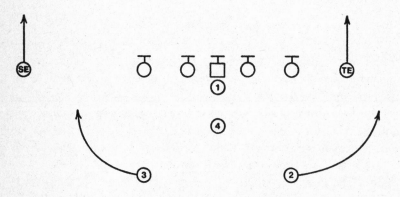

Diagram 5-24. 50 Quick

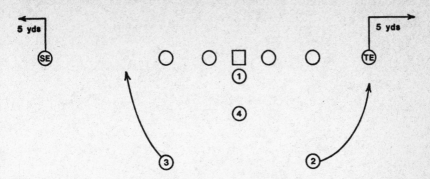

Diagram 5-25. 51 Quick Out

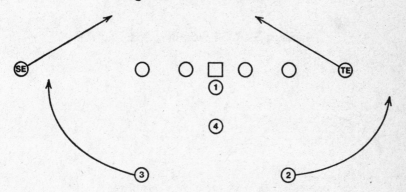

Diagram 5-26. 52 Quick Slant

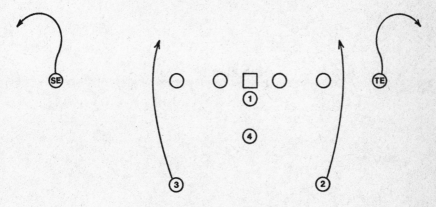

Diagram 5-27. 53 All Hook

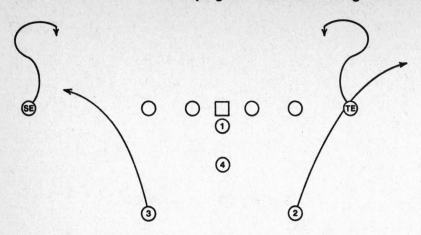

Diagram 5-28. 54 Sideline, Post, Turn In

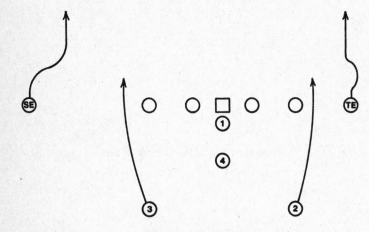

Diagram 5-29. 55

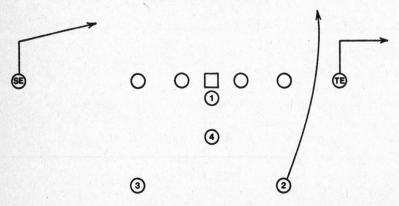

Diagram 5-30. 56

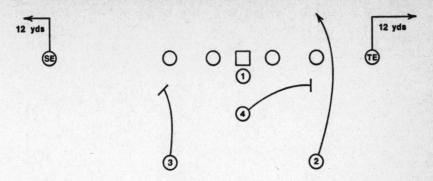

Diagram 5-31. 57

THE 60 HALFBACK MOTION SERIES

One of the most difficult problems for the defensive secondary is the use of motion by the offense. Motion causes the defense to make adjustments in a short period of time, so there are more chances for defensive errors. Motion legislates against the defensive coach's primary concern—to keep his people balanced, to keep from being outmanned in any one area. The 60 series gives the defense more to be concerned about, more to spend time on during the week's preparation. This means that less time can be spent in preparing for main areas where an offense excels.

The 60, 70 and 80 series give the offense an advantage because all are run with simple line blocking from the same basic offensive set. These passing series can be incorporated into a 2-minute offense, a catch-up offense, or a take-advantage offense when scouting reports indicate a defensive weakness. The 60 series plays are shown in Diagrams 5-32 through 5-35.

60 (Diagram 5-32)

SE: Runs waggle hook, 15 yards.

TE: Runs waggle bench, 12 yards.

FB: Goes in motion right. On count of "one-thousand-four," cuts upfield through cleared area.

RH: Sprints upfield 5 yards and bench.

LH: Blocks back to the weak side.

QB: Sprints straight back nine steps, sets up, checks cleared zone on motion side. Throws to fullback if open. If FB is not open,

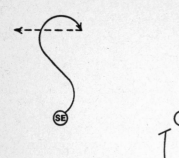
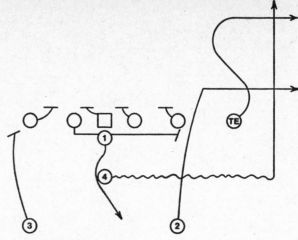

Diagram 5-32

hits SE on hook pattern. If SE has hooked, has line slide outside. If blitz comes, throws to short man.

RG: Pulls to the right and blocks first man to the outside.

RT: Blocks right if defense gaps, or blocks man over.

Line: Blocks down to the inside gap.

61 (Diagram 5-33)

SE: Runs waggle hook pattern 12 yards, then goes.

TE: Runs waggle outside 10 yards.

LH: Blocks back to weak side. Takes first man outside.

FB: Goes in motion. On four count, turns upfield and runs sprint pattern.

RH: Blocks outside. On two count, runs to cleared area in flat.

QB: Runs basic nine steps back, checks right side and hook man. Maybe pumps once on SE waggle hook and lofts ball for SE to run under. Second basic receiver is the delayed RH.

Line: Blocks inside seam.

RG: Pulls right and blocks first man to the outside. Drive block to reverse cut-off block.

LT: If defense gaps, he blocks right or blocks man over.

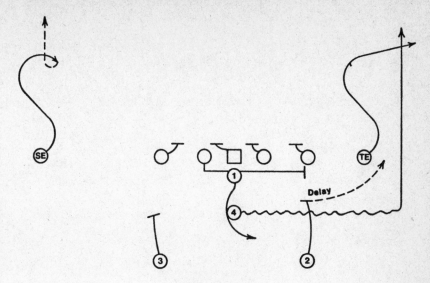

Diagram 5-33

62 (Diagram 5-34)

SE: Runs 10-yard waggle hook.

TE: Delay blocks for two count, then runs sprint pattern.

RH: Sprints 5-yard hook pattern.

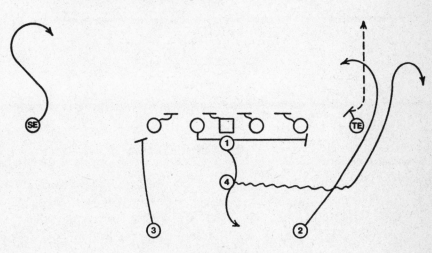

Diagram 5-34

FB: Goes in motion. On four count, runs 5-yard outside hook pattern.

LH: Blocks to weak side and takes first man outside.

RG: Pulls and blocks first man outside tackle.

LT: Blocks inside seam if man is there; if not, blocks man over.

Line: Blocks left inside shoulder gap.

All of the 60 series plays can be mirrored left by putting the fullback in motion to the left. The left halfback assumes the right halfback's duties, and the line blocks right if the defense gaps. The right guard would pull left and the right halfback would block the first man outside the right tackle (see Diagram 5-35 for the 62 Left).

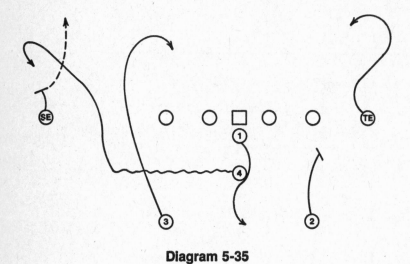

Diagram 5-35

THE 70 SERIES

The 70 series is designed to take advantage of the quickness of the fullback, of a possible crossbuck series, or of just the plain option. The 70 series can be run left or right. It gives you the full use of the Pro-Bone. See Diagrams 5-36 through 5-39.

70 (Diagram 5-36)

SE: Runs inside waggle post. Runs waggle 10 yards, and then cuts to sprint.

LH: Runs inside waggle flag. Runs waggle 8 yards and then cuts to sprint.

FB: Blocks first man outside of LT.

RH: Blocks first man outside of RT.

TE: Runs 10-yard waggle hook, slides sideline.

QB: Sprints back basic nine steps. Checks crossing pattern and looks to hook and slide.

Line: Uses cup block and forces defense outside.

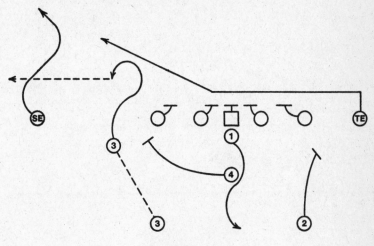

Diagram 5-36

71 (Diagram 5-37)

SE: Runs outside waggle flag.

LH: Runs outside waggle hook 6 yards, slides sideline.

TE: Runs down line of scrimmage 3 yards deep. Runs 8-yard flag sprint.

FB: Blocks first man outside of LT and hits cut-off block.

RH: Blocks first man outside of RT and hits drive outside.

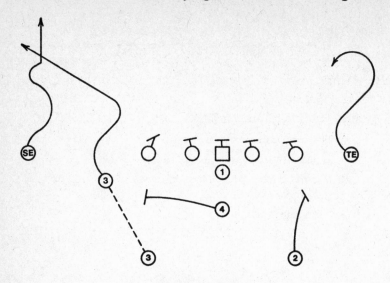

Diagram 5-37

QB: Sprints back 9 yards, checks LH hook slide, watches TE coming off cut.

Line: Uses cup block, forcing defense out and around.

72 Crossbuck (Diagram 5-38)

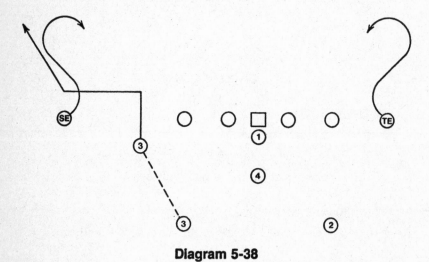

Diagram 5-38

SE: Runs inside waggle hook 12 yards.

LH: Runs sprint pattern sideline and up, and cuts behind SE.

FB: Uses crossbuck action. Makes good fake and blocks man in gap.

RH: Uses crossbuck action. Blocks man in gap 1 hole.

TE: Runs 10-yard inside waggle hook.

QB: Makes good crossbuck fake, sprints back 6 yards, fakes TE hook, watches LH sideline.

RG-RT: Block outside shoulder or man over.

LG-LT: Block outside shoulder or man over.

70 Series Flea-Flicker (Diagram 5-39)

The 70 Series Flea-Flicker can be run from this series.

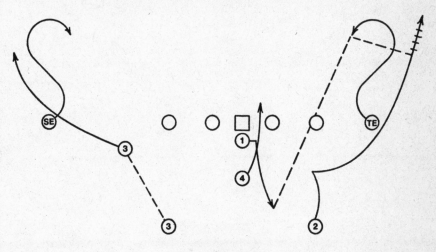

Diagram 5-39

THE 80 SERIES

The 80 series is an overload passing series. The objective is to bring about missed assignments in the defensive secondary. It is also effective when the defense has dropped off the line of scrimmage.

80 (Diagram 5-40)

SE: Fakes, stands up and goes.

TE: Runs outside waggle 10 yards and sprints for flag.

FB: Runs inside waggle 8 yards and sprints post.

LH: Goes in motion four counts and sprints sideline.

RH: Blocks outside man and releases to flat.

QB: Fakes, stands up and throws to SE. Sprints rollout to the right, 8 yards deep.

LT: Blocks inside gap.

LG: Pulls down line and blocks first man outside RT.

C/RG/RT: Block inside gap.

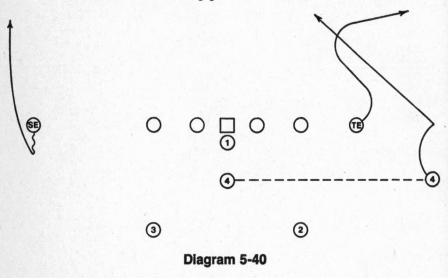

Diagram 5-40

81 (Diagram 5-41)

SE: Runs inside waggle 12 yards.

TE: Runs sprint out pattern.

FB: Runs sprint out pattern.

LH: Goes in motion four counts and runs sprint out pattern.

RH: Runs 10-yard sprint and bench pattern in cleared area.

LT: Blocks right shoulder gap.

C/RG/RT: Block left shoulder gap.

QB: From rollout action, sprints out 5 yards deep and hits first open man—LH is man most likely to be open.

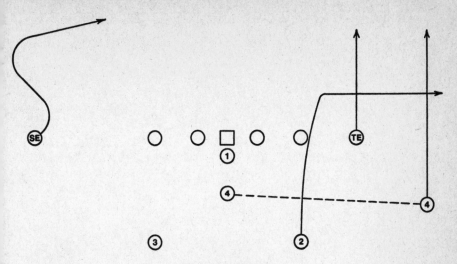

Diagram 5-41

6

Specialty Offenses

Specialty offenses keep defenses from stacking or overshifting. These offenses force the defense to stay home or face the threat of a quick score—the result of a defensive player being out of position.

Opposing coaches must spend valuable practice time preparing for these offenses. Special teams and special plays are thus very important, and they deserve important segments of your turnout schedule.

A good time to work on special plays is at the opening of practice, when players are usually confined to shorts, T-shirts, and football shoes. This puts the special plays and teams in their proper perspective as a critical part of the game. Later, Mondays and Thursdays can be used to implement and polish. These are non-contact days, and running the plays can be used for conditioning and loosening up.

The first plays to be presented are draw plays. Utilizing the talents of the running backs, these plays keep the defense from keying where they think a given play may be headed.

HB Draw—Two Back (Diagram 6-1)

The halfback draw is designed off the tackle trap. This is often a surprise because few teams use tackles to trap block.

SE: Runs deep post pattern.

LT: Pass blocks inside shoulder of defensive tackle, making him take an outside route—thus setting up the trap. After letting the defensive tackle slip outside, LT pass blocks the outside linebacker.

LG: Pass blocks the defensive man inside.

C : Pass blocks first man outside shoulder.

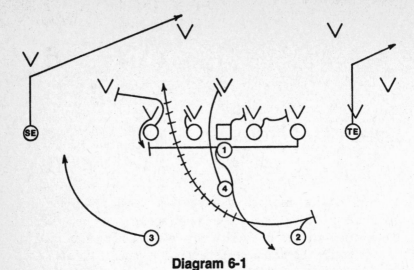

Diagram 6-1

RG: Pass blocks first man outside shoulder and looks for man over the tackle.

RT: Sets right foot forward, gives quick pass block look, then pulls inside arm technique.

TE: Runs deep flag pattern.

LH: Pass blocks, then flares to the outside.

FB: Takes a quick fake from QB, then goes through the line of scrimmage to block linebacker.

QB: Makes short fake to FB, then rolls out right and back. Hands off to the two back inside and continues pass action.

RH: Shows quick pass block, then steps to the inside, starting toward the 3 hole. Takes inside handoff from QB, follows the tackle and runs toward daylight.

HB Draw—Three Back (Diagram 6-2)

The Three Back HB Draw is run just opposite to the previous play.

Fullback Draw (Diagram 6-3)

The fullback draw lends itself well to the Pro-Bone because the fullback is so close to the quarterback. The guards should use short splits.

The center and guards pass block their men to the outside, the guards making contact with their shoulders to the inside armpits of

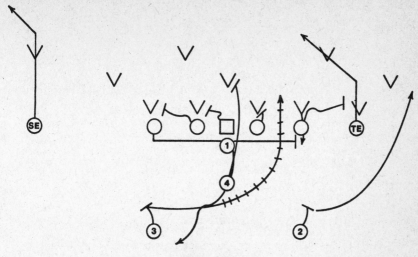

Diagram 6-2

the defensive men. They set with the inside foot, striking the blow with the arms together, turning the defensive man to the outside. Short, choppy steps are taken, letting the defensive man off the block to the outside. Guards must keep inside position for blocking angles, forcing the defensive people outside.

The quarterback must slip the ball into the stomach of the fullback (who is bent over), and continue sprinting back the way he would to throw a dropback pass.

The fullback stays over the ball for a "one-thousand-one, one-thousand-two" count, then runs up the middle.

After the guards have released their defensive men, they head up the field to block for the fullback.

SE: Sprints a slant-in pattern through the safety area.

LT: Pass blocks defensive man outside.

LG: Pass blocks using outside arm technique (see Diagram 6-3).

C: Shows pass block, and, after counting "one-thousand-one," blocks LB with pass block technique, shielding LB from FB.

RG: Same as LG, only in opposite direction.

RT: Pass blocks using outside arm technique.

TE: Runs deep flag pattern.

FB: In bent-over position, with arms up, lets QB slip the ball into the pocket area. After "one-thousand-one, one-thousand-two," follows the center and guards upfield.

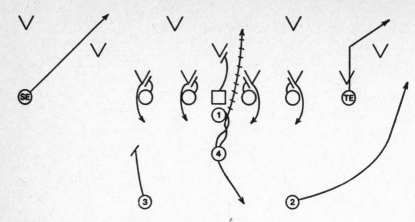

Diagram 6-3

QB: Pivots right and starts dropback pass action. Slips the ball to the FB as he goes by. Fakes passing action by sprinting back about 3 yards deeper than usual to set up.

LH: Pass blocks outside.

RH: Pass blocks outside, then flares out to act as secondary receiver.

Quarterback Draw (Diagram 6-4)

The quarterback draw is usually run from quick pass action. This is done so that the quarterback can show the ball quickly, making the defense read pass.

SE: Runs 52 slant.

LT: Pass blocks.

LG: Blocks first man inside.

C: Blocks first man inside.

RG: Trap blocks first man outside the center.

RT: Pass blocks.

TE: Runs 52 slant.

LH: Runs 52 pattern.

RH: Runs 52 pattern.

FB: Delays one count to let trapping guard by, then goes upfield to block for QB.

QB: Takes one step back, shows the ball as in 52 slant, then brings ball down and follows FB through the hole.

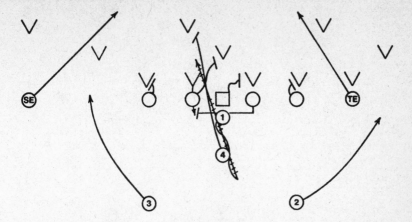

Diagram 6-4

Double Screen Pass (Diagram 6-5)

Another specialty play is the screen pass. In the Pro-Bone, the depth of the halfbacks helps in setting up the outside screen. The fake draw up the middle screen can be especially effective. The fullback is easy for the defensive linemen to lose because he is so close to the line of scrimmage.

SE: Runs deep sprint-out pattern.

RT: Holds pass block two counts, then doubles back as first man on screen wall.

RG: Holds pass block two counts, then doubles back as second man on screen wall.

C : Releases right after hiking ball and becomes third man on wall for two back.

LG: Comes to pass blocking position, then releases to far wall for three back.

LT: Comes to pass blocking position, then releases to form first position on screen wall for three back.

TE: Runs deep flag pattern.

FB: Pass blocks first man through without delaying him. Releases left to help form wall for three back. Looks for unoccupied defensive player or any who are reading screen; cut blocks any of these people.

RH: Fakes pass block, then moves over behind screen wall to look for pass.

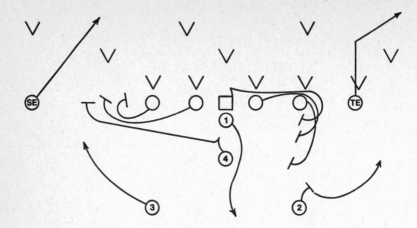

Diagram 6-5

LH: Holds two counts in pass block, then releases over to screen wall. Shouts "Go!" after ball is received.

QB: Sprints back deep—12 yards. Fakes to two back, drops back two steps more and throws to three back.

Center Screen (Diagram 6-6)

SE: Runs deep post pattern.

LT: Pass blocks, but lets man through and forms wall next to guard.

LG: Pass blocks, lets man through and forms wall next to center.

C: Pass blocks, then steps up to become first man on wedge.

RG: Pass blocks, letting man through and setting up next to center on screen wall.

RT: Pass blocks, then becomes third man right on screen wall.

TE: Runs deep post pattern.

LH: Runs flare pattern to draw corner out.

FB: Comes up between center and guard. Goes straight upfield looking for pass all the way.

RH: Steps outside for two counts, pass blocking, then comes back inside screen wall to receive pass. Shouts "Go!" when in control of ball.

QB: Makes short fake to FB, then takes deep 12-yard drop. Looks downfield, pumps once if he has time, then throws to two back behind the screen wall.

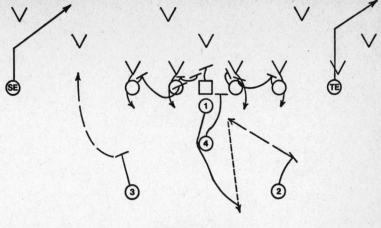

Diagram 6-6

The three plays that follow help to break up the rhythm of the offense. They represent situations that defenses must be aware of, and, hopefully, spend valuable time preparing for. These plays can be put in on Thursday night, when the teams are running the offense up and down the field for timing. These effective plays are the Flea-Flicker (Diagram 6-7), the Double Pass (Diagram 6-8), and the Statue Left (Diagram 6-9).

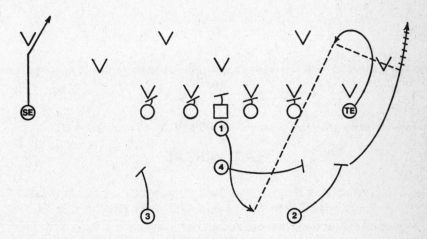

Diagram 6-7

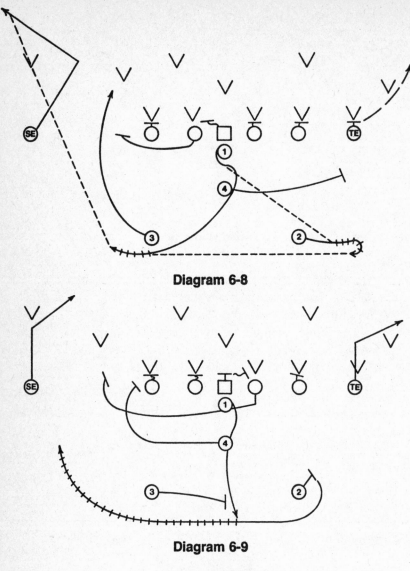

Diagram 6-8

Diagram 6-9

LONG YARDAGE

This section deals with situations in which a score is needed from long range—from your own 5 yard line to the opponent's 30 yard line. In these situations, defenses will allow the short gain, but not the long, quick touchdown. Most defenses will shift a man to the wide side of the field. The following pass patterns should be effective in these situations:

51	92	84 Special
53 All Hook	70	FB Draw
57	60 Right and Left	FB Center Screen
90	81	Rollout right flood pattern

These patterns take advantage of a drop-off defense. Short hooks can also be used to set up the flea-flicker.

Receivers are instructed to get out of bounds quickly when they see that they can't advance the ball further downfield. If they are tackled in bounds, the quarterback should line the team up quickly and run a play.

In this situation, the best play could be the quick bench pattern off the regular offense. The quarterback can go on the first sound after the set color play. Thursday practice is a good time to prepare for this type of situation.

At these practices, the offense can run plays up and down the field. You provide the down and situation. The offense should practice running back to the line of scrimmage and throwing the quick bench. Should the quarterback want to change the play, this can be done by the number right after the color. The team will know they will run the 51 bench if the clock does not stop. But, if the quarterback says 53 or 92 after the color, they should be able to change the pattern.

The 84 Right (Diagram 6-10) and the 84 Left (Diagram 6-11) offer other ways to line up the 80 series, and are useful in the situations we've been describing.

If the time is under 60 seconds and a receiver stays in bounds, time out should be called immediately.

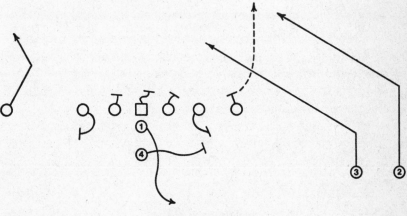

Diagram 6-10

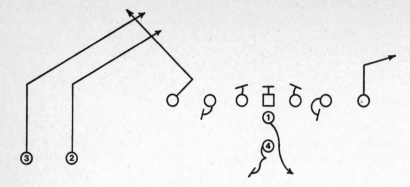

Diagram 6-11

SHORT YARDAGE

These plays apply when the offense has the ball on or inside the opponent's 30 yard line. When you are in field goal range, location of the ball must be kept in mind when selecting plays.

Unless the offense has all its timeouts left, the passing game must be utilized to control the clock. Play action can be used, and screens, the statue, and the double pass are effective in this area, as are the following:

51	71	Quick pitch passes
52	61	Crossbuck pass
58	62	27-36 Sweep pass
57	80	2 Back motion, fake lead
90 Roll out right or left flood	84	Option pass

The Pattern 90 Right can be changed to a tight end post 15 yards and hook. This puts the tight end behind the linebacker drop zone and brings him back toward the ball (see Diagram 6-12).

This type of pattern will keep the ball in midfield. A fullback flea-flicker can also be run off this pattern.

Running to the short side of the field means that backs can get out of bounds more quickly. When running the flood rollout right, the halfback, if he can delay one or two counts, will come in behind the defensive end or corner.

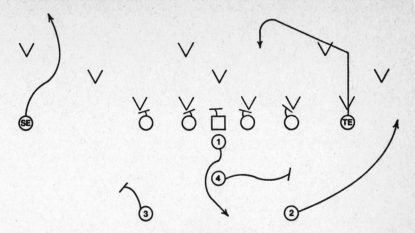

Diagram 6-12

GOAL LINE OFFENSE

The rule inside the 10 yard line should be to always close the gaps down to keep the defense from penetrating. Since the size of the playing area is reduced, the defense has less area to cover.

When the defense gaps, the fullback trap is often effective, or the fullback can block the first free man to the outside. See the 36, illustrated in Diagram 6-13.

A double tight end alignment can also be used to add strength to the weakside running game. Halfbacks in the Pro-Bone, because of their deep set, can more easily read what the defense is doing. The 36 can be run with wedge blocking as in Diagram 6-14.

The wedge is formed on the offensive man who plays where the play will go. The blockers on either side come across the defensive men, driving their shoulder pads behind the lead blockers' arms. The force of the charge must be sufficient to force any low defensive back out of position. See Diagram 6-15.

The two back takes the first man outside, with the fullback sealing the inside. The two back and the fullback can change assignments, creating a cross block with good angle (Diagram 6-16).

On the wedge block, the rest of the line must seal block to the inside gap of where the play is being run (see the Wedge 34, in Diagram 6-17).

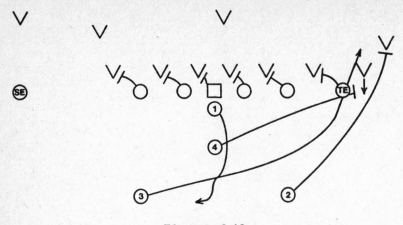

Diagram 6-13

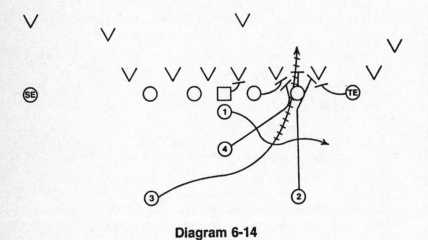

Diagram 6-14

From the wedge series the quarterback can keep the ball after faking to the three back on the 34-36, and throw to the tight end coming off his block.

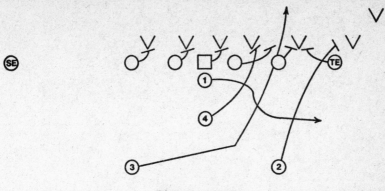

Diagram 6-15

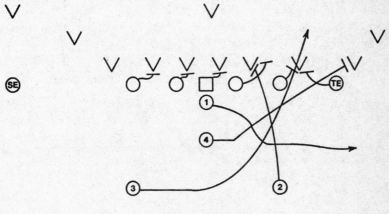

Diagram 6-16

These are plays for the 10-yard offense:

51	Quick pitch pass
52	Lead options
Flood right and left	Regular options
90 series or rollout	outside pitch
QB sprint out right or left	Power sweeps and
Quick pitch 39 or 28	HB pass

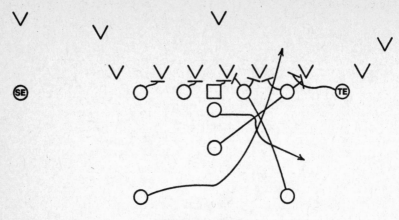

Diagram 6-17

In some states, tie ball games are decided by giving each team four downs to score from the opponent's 10 yard line. This makes it doubly important that the 10-yard offense be included in the week's preparation.

The plays in this chapter can be modified, with individual patterns and running lanes changed to suit your personnel.

7

Coaching the
Pro-Bone Fundamentals

The title for this chapter is general for what we consider to be a good reason: Many "basics" are necessary in order to put the Pro-Bone into operation, and we have chosen to include as many of those basics as we can in one place.

Coaching fundamentals are covered, starting with the organization of turnouts, basics of each backfield position, stances, pass routes, cadence, the huddle—and so on, including coaching for specific problem areas that the offense may encounter.

Achieving success requires attention to details. While player ability is important, coaching the fundamentals that complement both that ability and a given offensive system is also critical. Time and the size of your staff affect the amount of detailed work that can be done. Regardless of size, all staffs should select goals that are reasonable. Coaches should be used efficiently, with responsibilities delegated to reflect their areas of strength.

Before detailed coaching work begins, a schedule such as this one should be set up for the week's practice:

Game Plan for the Week of _____

Offensive Game Plans

I. Weakness of opponent's defense

    A. Type of defense opponent plays: _____

B. List of weaknesses in scouting report:

1. _____
2. _____
3. _____
4. _____

C. Strengths of opponent's defense:

1. _____
2. _____
3. _____

D. Plays that should be worked on during week to beat opponent's defense:

1. _____ 3. _____ 5. _____ 7. _____
2. _____ 4. _____ 6. _____ 8. _____

E. Pass offense pattern to be worked on during week:

1. _____ 3. _____ 5. _____
2. _____ 4. _____ 6. _____

F. Two-minute offense plays:

1. _____ 3. _____ 5. _____
2. _____ 4. _____ 6. _____

G. Goal line offense:

1. _____ 3. _____ 5. _____
2. _____ 4. _____ 6. _____

H. Special plays to be used during the game:

1. _____ 3. _____
2. _____ 4. _____

I. Substitutions for offensive game: _____

J. Special substitutions:

1. Goal line offense _____
2. Two-minute offense _____
3. Kicking game _____

K. Catch-up offense: _____

L. Ball-control offense: _____

Defensive Game Plans

I.   Type of offense opponent runs: _____

II.   Strengths of opponent's offense:

        1. _____

        2. _____

        3. _____

        4. _____

III.   Exceptional ball players:

        1. _____   3. _____

        2. _____   4. _____

IV.   Type of defenses to prepare during practice week:

        1. _____   3. _____

        2. _____   4. _____

V.   Special defenses for blocking the punt and extra point: _____

        _____

VI.   Substitution for the game: _____

VII.   Special substitution for goal line defense or prevent defense:

        _____

VIII. Special plays defense must be aware of: _____

IX.   Sideline communications to field: _____

X.   List of special teams: _____

XI.   Opponent's kickoff and punt averages: _____

XII.   Special kickoff and punt plays: _____

XIII. Pre-game checklist: _____

XIV. Halftime order of events: _____

     This represents a structure within which detailed coaching work can be done, both on the skills required to operate the Pro-Bone smoothly and to prepare for specific problems. Here now, position by position, are things that players need to learn how to do.

Quarterback

    1. When receiving the ball from the center, the QB should use the open-hand, thumbs together approach. The right hand should be tight into the crack of the center so that the latter feels the pres-

sure. The right hand should be spread with the thumb pointing down the inside of the center's leg. The back of the left hand should be against the center's leg and the hand should be spread, with the left thumb touching the right. When the ball is snapped, the center feels the pressure of the right hand to guide the ball properly. The left hand collapses around the ball, ensuring full control.

2. The QB takes a quarter turn when operating the option left or right. He shows the ball to the fullback's stomach, brings it back into his side, completes another half turn, then moves in a straight line toward the halfback.

3. The QB shows the ball to the halfback's stomach, and rides one or two steps with him.

4. Disengaging the ball from the halfback's stomach, the QB brings the ball to his own stomach area with two hands.

5. The pitch to the halfback is a one-handed push of the football, making it turn end-over-end for the flare back to receive.

6. The QB should always be parallel to the line of scrimmage and going upfield, never away from the line of scrimmage.

7. The QB read on the tackle, which determines the handoff to the halfback, is usually the hardest for the QB to master. Large sections of drill time should be spent on this early in the season. The key is how far the tackle has moved the defensive player off the line of scrimmage.

Halfback

1. The HB should be about 4½ yards deep. This position can be adjusted—forward to make up for slowness, backward to take advantage of speed.

2. The weight on the hand of the halfback should not be heavy. The weight should be on the instep of the foot.

3. The head must always look straight ahead. This enables the HB to watch the block of the tackle in front of him, showing him which path he should take.

4. When the option HB flares to the outside, he must be deep enough to have outside leverage on the defensive end. The flare back should never be shallow. The deep position makes containment of the defense easier. Furthermore, the depth of his position makes it easier for the flare back to look the pitched football into his hands before he attempts to cut.

5. Halfbacks should always listen carefully to spacing instructions in the huddle, so that they line up properly in relation to the tackles.

Fullback

1. The fullback should have his weight forward and be directly behind the QB.

2. The FB blocking technique, outside the filling of the guard position, is that of a pulling guard and should be taught that way. The FB changes direction by bringing the arm in the direction he is pulling, directly to that side's hip. The elbow is tucked tight to the hip, causing body weight to be shifted toward the desired direction. Bringing in the elbow just below the hip helps to keep the head down. As the elbow is being tucked in, the foot on that side turns in the desired direction. The other foot is then brought up. The body has a low profile and good momentum.

Here are special areas that players will have to work on.

BALL EXCHANGE AND FAKING

The FB should create an open pocket with stomach open, arms up, and elbows out. To do this, backs should learn the following: Taking the first step toward the hole, the back raises both elbows and slips his hands under them, then locks his fingers in the up position. This opens the stomach area and brings the head up. The QB now has an open area to place the ball and draw it back.

When the QB hands off, the back wraps his fingers around the ends of the football. This minimizes the possibility of a fumble, should the back be hit shortly after taking the handoff. When the ball is given or faked to the back, his head comes down, completing a good fake. Handoff technique with all backs is the same, but the fullback should hold the ball with hands over both ends of the ball until he breaks beyond the LB area. The HB shifts the ball to either side, cutting off the block by the tackle. The HB grasps the ball when he feels it left in his stomach after one step. The open pocket technique gives the QB time to withdraw the ball because of the time lag between the halfback's coming over the ball and grasping both ends.

If the backs do not receive the ball, they should act as if they do have it. Movement of the head and shoulders down as if to grab the ball helps hold the linebacker longer, cutting down pursuit.

After the QB has shown the ball in the pocket of the FB, he returns it back into his own stomach area. He uses both hands, ensuring good control of the ball as he turns to go parallel to the line of scrimmage and make contact with the HB.

The two-handed method also helps the QB direct the ball in his pitch.

BACKFIELD SPACING AND ALIGNMENT

The backfield spacing and alignment of the Pro-Wishbone provide the following advantages for running backs:

1. The depth allows time for a good read on the offensive lineman's block.
2. Backs can get outside quickly on pitches and pass patterns.
3. Depth provides ease on sweep action for cutting into proper running lanes.
4. Defensive problems are caused by a back always going in counter motion to the play action.
5. The defense can't stack to a strong side because of the balanced backfield.
6. The weak side can be attacked as easily as the strong side.

The backfield depth should be adjusted to the personnel you have available. To adjust for proper spacing, line up the backfield without the line.

Lay out the running lanes (Diagram 7-1) with chalk. With the center and the backs, run the options left and right. Adjust the halfbacks forward or back depending on the time it takes the quarterback to reach the halfback after the fake to the fullback.

The fullback should come forward from a three-point stance,

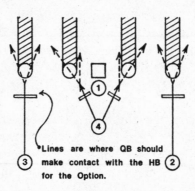

Diagram 7-1

raising up slightly. The fullback's hands should be locked under his elbows, with his stomach open for the quarterback to place the ball. This is important because the quarterback has to be able to withdraw the ball without interference from the fullback. The quarterback can use a hand fake for greater speed, allowing him to get to the halfback more quickly. The fullback must come over the ball and a good fake must be made to hold the linebackers.

The halfbacks come forward, heads up, looking at the angle of the block being made by the tackle. When the quarterback engages him—when he feels the ball—he continues forward two steps and makes his cut off the tackle's block. During the two-step ride, the quarterback also reads the block and makes his decision to hand off or keep. If he keeps, he options the defensive end for the keep, or pitches to the trailing halfback.

HALFBACK BACKFIELD SPACING

Running the split backfield requires that halfbacks be adjusted inside and moved up. The gaps of the guards and tackles have to be adjusted accordingly, to 2 feet for guards and 4 feet for the tackles. The halfbacks line up in the gaps of the tackles. This enables the quarterback to fake better, and makes handing off easier. The split end maintains the 4-yard split, keeping the defensive man with him.

This split back set can be used effectively by playing a split end or other good receiver in the fullback position. See Diagram 7-2.

Using the regular set, backs can be adjusted in the following ways to facilitate ball handling and quickness:

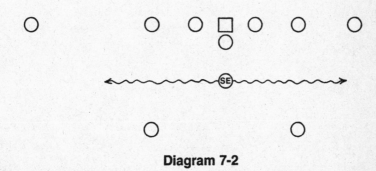

Diagram 7-2

1. Move the halfbacks to 3 yards from the line of scrimmage.
2. To enable backs to hit holes more quickly, cut down the ride time on the fake. The halfback should come over the ball with a pocket.

Moving the backs closer does not change the offense. It is an adjustment that compensates for lack of speed or the ability to hit the hole and run to daylight. It is also an adjustment for muddy fields where footing is a problem.

This does make it difficult for the halfback to read the block of the tackle. The halfback goes to the inside hip of the offensive tackle and runs a dive action. Wedge blocking can be used to help the halfback.

FULLBACK SPACING

When backs are spaced in the usual way, the fullback can be adjusted 3 feet further back from the quarterback. See Diagram 7-3.

A fullback option can be run from this set: The quarterback opens up on a full pivot on his right foot, stepping back toward the fullback. When the ball is engaged with the fullback's stomach, the quarterback gives just a one-step ride, allowing the fullback to take the direction dictated by the blocks of the guards and center. The quarterback must then complete the full turn and sprint down the line of scrimmage to meet the halfback coming through the hole. In this case, the halfbacks must be adjusted back ¾ yard to allow for the longer fake to the fullback. See Diagram 7-4.

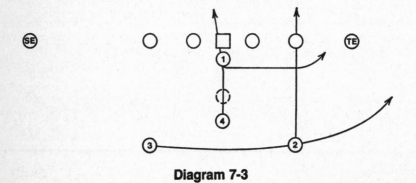

Diagram 7-3

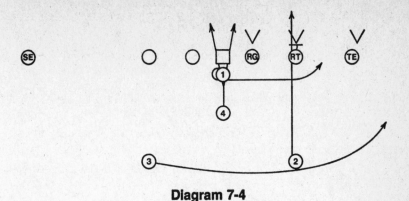

Diagram 7-4

LINE SPACING

This discussion of the advantages of short and wide line spacing will include, as well, details of blocking strategy and technique.

The quarterback determines line spacing to set up certain plays, or sometimes to see how the defense is going to react to a particular alignment. Short spacing is effective on power plays or 34-23 leads. If the defense tightens in response, the quick pitch opens up. Wide spacing creates good running lanes for the fullback if the defensive tackles or guards adjust to the offensive tackles. The nose guard can be double-teamed and, because the fullback is so close to the line of scrimmage, he is usually through the hole and into the secondary before the defense can react. If the defense lines up in the gaps, the offensive line can block down for a gap defense, and the fullback blocks the first loose man to the outside. This creates good running lanes for the halfbacks.

The key to using the different splits effectively is mastery of the technique of blocking gaps with good, aggressive cut-off blocks. Drills can be used with the quarterback and fullback, in which the guards block different defensive alignments and the fullback practices cutting off their blocks. With a 10-minute drill each practice period, the line learns quickly to adjust to various defenses. Linemen should be asked to create various situations in their minds. They can block for these different situations, in their heads at least, while they await their turns in drills. This mental activity should be stressed. It may be done for ten minutes before bed, during blackboard sessions—any time.

STANCES

The three-point stance for linemen is recommended for the following reasons:

1. The body can be in a relaxed position, yet remain explosive—the lineman can get off the line quickly.
2. The head can be held up more easily, allowing better eye contact on the defensive man.
3. Body balance is better, making pulling out and cut-off blocking easier.
4. There is more foot contact with the ground for better driving power (an analogy to car tires could be made: the more tire surface on the road, the more traction and power).

The three-point stance is taught by having the player stand normally, with the outsides of the feet even with the outsides of the shoulders. Have the player jump up and down, moving the feet out a few inches beyond the shoulders until it feels comfortable. When a comfortable spread is found, the right foot should be moved back until the toes are even with the instep of the left foot. The player can then squat down to a comfortable level with his left elbow resting on his left knee. The right hand is placed forward on the ground and some weight is placed on it. The buttocks stay higher than the head. The position must be comfortable, but a weight shift must also be possible without defensive players detecting it and keying in on it. Thus, the lineman maintains a good, comfortable strike position as he listens to the quarterback, particularly for hot colors indicating a play change on the line of scrimmage. The lineman's neck is pulled back and his head is up.

Different stances must sometimes be used.

The tackle's main responsibility is blocking the man over him. The defensive man must be kept from penetrating—the tackle must control him on the line of scrimmage. This means that the tackle must get off the ball quickly, so for this type of blocking the tackle should use the four-point stance. This keeps his weight forward and enables him to drive hard off the ball. The option block by the tackle is a hard drive block, so again he is aided by the four-point stance.

These stance changes enhance the entire offense in that blocking assignments are more likely to be carried out efficiently when they are prepared for in terms of specific techniques. Besides the knowledge of the snap count, they are an additional advantage that the linemen have over the defense.

The three-point stance is probably most desirable for receivers. Balance is better, causing a quicker yet more controlled release off the line of scrimmage. It could also be more comfortable, and it's easier for the receiver to look in and see the snap of the ball. Split ends can stand up if it feels more natural, but time is lost coming off the line of scrimmage by doing so. Ends should be timed for depth of patterns as well as for how long it takes them to cover the various routes. This is done, of course, so that the quarterback will know where they are on given plays. The more the quarterback knows, the more confident he becomes; and the more confidence he has in throwing the ball, the better for the offense.

When you work with ends, time the patterns and the total completion time. This helps the receiver know where he should be and when to look for the ball. Have receivers count "one thousand one, one thousand two . . .," so that they learn to look at the right time and go for the ball. Most coaches teach receivers to go for the ball, but if the receiver looks before the ball comes, he loses speed, he loses direction, and he loses his advantage over the defensive man. Once he does look for the ball, of course, the receiver should look it all the way into his hands.

The quarterback, since he knows the receivers' routes and how long it takes to run them, should be able to do a better job of setting up, looking at secondary receivers, and then throwing to the primary receiver. If possible, in the off season, quarterbacks and receivers should be reminded to visualize routes and passes, so that their minds at least are continually going over them. There is little time to think in game situations. Those who react rather than think usually win ball games, so anything done to make pass patterns become second nature will help. Players should be taught to do their thinking ahead of time—thinking up different situations and counters that may occur—so that they learn to react quickly under pressure.

With the regular Pro-Bone option pass series, line blocking is from short and regular spacing to cut down blocking area. The Pro-Bone option pass series, on the other hand, consists of the short patterns that are thrown from the basic running option plays. Keys are given by the split end, either off the line or in the huddle. See Diagram 7-5.

As shown in the diagram, potential coverages of the split end

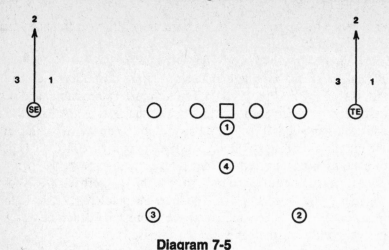

Diagram 7-5

are numbered. The split end can call the coverage on specific patterns if the quarterback wishes, or simply give the coverage on the way into the huddle. The quarterback calls the color, then a number, pauses for the split end to call the coverage, and then calls the cadence. All numbered patterns can be changed to individual patterns such as option right, tight end bench and go.

The three-point stance is probably desirable for linemen as well as receivers. Direction changes are made easier and it is also easier to hide balance changes in the three-point stance. The four-point stance keeps weight forward, over the hips, affecting the head and shoulders, making it more difficult to pick up blitzes. This is especially important, given the wide gaps utilized in the Pro-Bone. When teaching linemen their stances, teach right-side linemen to keep their feet outside shoulders width, left foot forward, the toe of the right foot matching the left instep. Left-side linemen do the opposite: right foot forward, toe of left foot matching right instep.

Linemen should touch the ground with extended fingers. The head is more flexible in this position and vision forward is accomplished with less strain. This position is also more comfortable, and the more comfortable linemen are as the cadence is counted, the better.

The center should deliver the ball to the quarterback so that the strings fit the quarterback's right hand (if the quarterback is right-handed, of course). He holds the ball this way as he carries out his faking, needing only to slide his hand down the ball and throw when the time comes.

On the basic option, the quarterback always reverse pivots. He turns toward the fullback and makes a short fake because the fullback is so close. The quarterback continues his pivot until he faces down the line. When throwing off the run option, he must also give a short fake to the halfback. He exposes the ball, draws it back in, moves to the outside. He throws to the intended receiver from this outside position. The ball should be thrown with the weight on the back foot and the hips in front of the arm. Good follow-through is extremely important.

BLOCKING

We turn our attention now to more detailed concerns involving blocking. When defenses change between downs, a count-off blocking system can be used. Count-off blocking must be used when defenses blitz or overload offensive linemen. Starting with the center, who is numbered 0, defensive people are numbered as follows: The first man to the right of the center is 1, the next man 2, and so on (see Diagram 7-6). When using this system, offensive linemen know what their responsibilities are, regardless of what the defense does—regardless of the number of defensive men on the line of scrimmage. Each offensive lineman's responsibility is to block the first man to the inside or the man over. Penetration to the inside must be cut off.

As a rule, the center's responsibility is to block the immediate man over or the man in the gap away from the play. Count-off blocking is facilitated by appropriate play selection. Leads, power plays and quick pitches are usually effective.

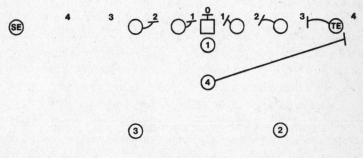

Diagram 7-6

LEAD BLOCKING

Lead blocking is usually done by the fullback and guards. Effective lead blocks are those in which the offensive player explodes through the defensive man and drives him backward—hopefully taking him off his feet. We will discuss four different lead blocks:

1. The blocker drives through the defensive man, striking the blow with the shoulder. The arm is rotated into the man, creating a blocking line composed of arm, shoulder and head. With movement from the hips, extension of the legs and rotation of the arm, the blocker's weight is propelled forward to maximum advantage.

2. The blocker drives low, coming up at the last second into the man's chest, driving him backward.

3. The blocker aims high toward the chest, and at the last second goes toward the instep of the foot, cutting the man down.

4. The blocker drives through the man, as in the first lead block above, then goes into a reverse cut-off block, putting his body between the defensive man and the ball carrier. Once into the crab cut-off block, the blocker continues crabbing into the man.

INDIVIDUAL BLOCKING ASSIGNMENTS

The key to effective blocking for the option is that the linemen stay with their blocking assignments. The blocker must make contact in a controlled manner, staying on his feet and using the defensive man's weight to the blocker's advantage. Blockers should be taught to explode through the defensive man, **head up**, extending the legs and hips and rotating the arms in a continuous motion. The feet should take short, continuous steps. If the blocker starts to lose the defensive man, he should go with the direction of the defensive player's charge, staying with him. The lineman should go into a crab cut-off block, always pushing his body into the defensive man. The depth of the backs makes cut-off blocking easier.

The guards are taught to use these four types of blocks on linebackers. Pulling guards are taught the following: From the three-point stance, with weight evenly distributed, the guard steps in the direction he is to pull—a short jab step. In the same motion—in fact, to start the motion—the guard, if he is pulling right, jerks his right elbow into his right hip. This causes his body weight to gain momentum in the pulling direction, and keeps the head and shoulders down. The foot should be parallel to the line of scrimmage, not back from the line of scrimmage. After the short jab step with the right foot, the weight should be on it and the left foot should be brought forward. A continuous motion down the line is then made, with a good wide base maintained for blocking.

Pulling to the left is just the opposite, with the pull starting with the left foot, the left elbow going into the left side. The guard pulling drill can be used for four minutes a day to improve technique and quickness.

BLOCKING THE BLITZ AND CHANGING DEFENSES

In blocking the blitz, the main objective is to cover the inside gaps. If a team you are to play blitzes or changes defenses frequently, attention should be paid during practice week to plays that utilize the fullback blocking, and to the quarterback calling such plays as quick pitches, stand up passes, power plays and leads. Linemen cover the inside gaps, with the fullback picking up the first man to the outside. If plays are used that get the ball outside, the defense can't keep coming. The use of different splits on the line of scrimmage also makes the defensive man pay attention to where he must play. If he doesn't, good gains are made, and defensive coaches must make adjustments. Quick cadences and a silent count can be used to further confuse the defense.

The best remedy for blitzes and changing defenses is the practice time that is spent in preparing for them. The wedge block with lead blocking can be used to great advantage and will be discussed more fully. While preparing in practice for teams that blitz and change defenses, you should remember that the Pro-Bone has built-in defenses against these tactics: First, it is hard to overload because it is run from an even set. Second, there is no defensive area that can't be attacked (and, to return to our first point, defenses become particularly vulnerable in some areas if they overload others). Third, advantages come from the good blocking angles provided by the splits discussed earlier.

Practice against blitzes and changing defenses should include emphasis on blocking technique, particularly double-team blocking and wedge blocking.

DOUBLE-TEAM BLOCKING

The double team can be taught this way: One offensive man takes the defensive man head on, taking away his momentum. The outside blocker then seals the man to keep him from rolling outside the block. If the defense stunts outside, the outside man takes away the defensive man's charge and the inside man seals, as shown in Diagram 7-7. If the defensive man is in the gap, then the tackle and the tight end must attack shoulder to shoulder, keeping their hips together, and drive the man back. The hips must be together so that the double team can't be split.

Diagram 7-7

WEDGE BLOCKING

The wedge block is accomplished by three blockers forming a V. The blocker on the running lane leads and the other linemen are behind him with their heads approximately at his shoulder pads. The lead man drives into the defensive man, and then goes into a four-point run-off block. The other blockers also go to the four-point run-off block. The blockers must take short jabbing steps and keep pressure forward. The rearward blockers should stay close to the lead blocker, pressuring with their heads and shoulder pads, so that the defensive player must slide to the outside. See Diagrams 7-8 and 7-9. The closeness of the fullback to the line of scrimmage helps to form the wedge quickly. This seals off any quick penetration by a blitzing linebacker.

The lead blocking halfback is also important. He must block aggressively the first loose defensive man, or fill any holes left. If the V is formed, the lead back adds further momentum to the lead man in the V. If the lead blocker breaks through the wedge, he should continue downfield and block the first loose man.

We now turn to specialty blocks and blocking situations which become necessary when encountering defensive problems with the Pro-Bone.

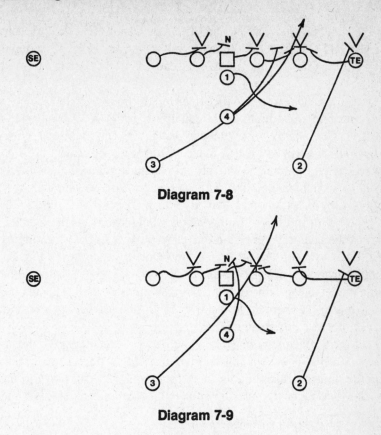

Diagram 7-8

Diagram 7-9

SPECIALTY BLOCKS

These blocks are to be used in addition to the straight-on, shoulder block.

1. *Cut-off block*: This is a filling block, in which the lineman comes down the line of scrimmage, head pointed to the outside hip of the defensive player. The blocker drives through the defensive player with his body and shoulder, turning him in the direction of the force of his head. With short, choppy steps, the blocker drives the defensive player down the line of scrimmage, keeping him from penetrating.

2. *Reverse cut-off block*: The blocker drives a shoulder block into the defensive man to stop his momentum, then goes to the left or right, depending on which way the ball carrier is to run or which area is to be protected. From the shoulder block, the blocker pivots

on the shoulder, moving leg and hips behind the defensive man as in a cross body. This keeps the defensive man from quick pursuit and makes him grab for the runner instead of getting set for a good tackle.

3. *Climb block*: The blocker advances into his man, shoulder blocking him waist high. After contact is made, the blocker starts his shoulder climbing up the defensive man's body, toward his chest. The moment contact is made, the upward movement must be started. The right leg steps into the man, forcing the blocker's back to straighten up. The left foot is brought up immediately, followed by short, choppy steps that keep the momentum forward.

4. *California block*: In this block, the blocker uses the momentum of the charging defensive player to move him out of a running lane or away from the QB when the latter is passing. The blocker comes toward the defensive man, and as soon as contact is made, he turns immediately in the direction of the defensive man. The blocker thus adds his momentum to the direction of the defensive player and drives him out of the running or passing area.

5. *Downfield run-off block*: The blocker runs down the defensive man, always keeping his eyes on him and his body between him and the runner. Under control at all times and with feet moving, the blocker is able to change direction with the defensive player and shield the latter from the play.

HALFBACK RUNNING PATTERNS

1. The HB in running the option must come off the snap signal hard with his head up, trying to read the tackle's block. He takes two steps, raises his elbows, and watches what is happening ahead. When he feels the football, he comes down over it. If the ball is given, he takes it to the side opposite his cut off the tackle's block. If he has kept his head up properly, he should have a good perspective on how he will run and cut.

2. When the HB comes out of the backfield on a pass pattern, he comes at full speed, flaring to the outside. This provides outside leverage and less chance of being caught or held up at the line of scrimmage. It also forces the defensive secondary to adjust more quickly. This enables the QB to get a better read on his pass patterns.

3. There is an exception to the rule about coming out of the

backfield quickly. On the delayed halfback pass, the HB receiving the ball fakes a block first, then comes out hard. This usually creates coverage by a defensive corner or linebacker, which is likely to be a mismatch in the offense's favor.

THE MOVING POCKET FOR PASS OFFENSE

Some defensive problems can be resolved by the use of a moving pocket.

1. The straight-ahead blocking that is needed for pass protection is harder to employ now in high school ball because of limitations on use of the head in blocking. Striking the first blow with the shoulders, it is more difficult to maintain squared-off contact with the defensive ball player. The shoulder pass block can be used, but changing the blocking for pass offense helps keep the defense off balance. Diagram 7-10 shows the moving pocket right, and Diagram 7-11 shows the moving pocket left.

2. The key to the moving pocket is that the linemen get good angle shoulder blocks. They are meeting defensive players from the side and have generated momentum.

3. The center and fullback must keep the defensive men from tailgating and linebackers must be kept from blitzing between the moving linemen.

4. The QB in the dropback offense must now sprint to his position, left or right, setting up the required 7 to 9 yards deep. Sprinting enables him to get to his set-up position quickly.

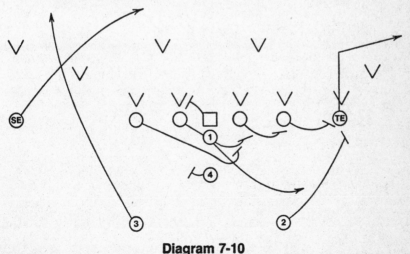

Diagram 7-10

Diagram 7-11

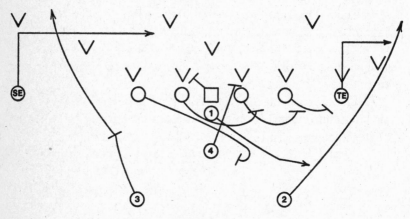

Diagram 7-12

5. Four-man patterns are set up the same way, except that the strongside HB checks for blitzing men before releasing to his pass pattern. As Diagram 7-12 shows, the protection is more than adequate.

DOUBLE TIGHT END

In order to provide additional strength to the split end side, a double tight end formation can be used. Should a tight-end-size person not be available, the split end can move in. For variety, he can start out at the weakside tight end, then flex out after the cadence starts.

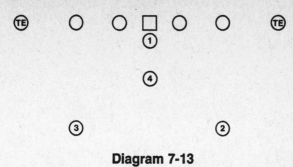

Diagram 7-13

When a smaller player is used at tight end, he should use angle and cross block techniques to help him handle his assignment. For additional help in a situation like this, motion of the halfback and then a double team with him on the defensive end can be utilized.

The left tight end still uses the normal split of 3 to 5 yards from the tackle (see Diagram 7-13). From this position, the split end and tight ends can run delay patterns off backfield motion or quick outs. They can also run end-arounds or double reverses.

BLOCKING THE WIDE 38 SWEEP

The Inside 36 Sweep is one of the bread-and-butter plays of the Pro-Bone and it usually enjoys considerable success. Sometimes, however, it becomes difficult to keep the defensive end from stringing out the play.

Moving the tight end in to a 1½-yard split is a possible solution, but the end still seems to have leverage. Furthermore, bringing the tight end in could give a key to the defense, even though a quick pitch off this set could neutralize that potential advantage.

The defensive end must be sealed so that the guard can get upfield. Another solution is to use the three back to double-team the end, but this still does not present the ideal solution.

This seems to be the best solution: The three back or the fullback can be put in motion without losing power on the sweep. If a stand-off block can be obtained from the tight end, the defensive end can be neutralized—he can be stood up and kept parallel to the line of scrimmage. Pass blocking this way enables the motion man to seal the corner without clipping the defensive end.

Thus, tight ends should be coached to pass block the end, keeping the latter from penetrating and keeping him parallel to the

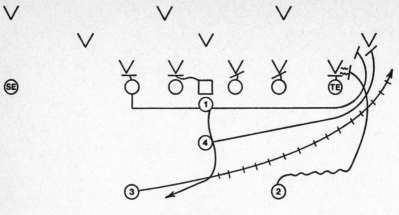

Diagram 7-14

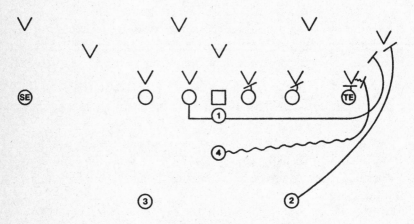

Diagram 7-15

line of scrimmage. Diagram 7-14 illustrates the Three Back Block. In Diagram 7-15, the Fullback Motion Block is shown.

As the diagrams show, the motion man seals with a pass block at a right angle to the tight end. A solid stopper is created that keeps the defense from pursuing down the line of scrimmage. The motion man executing this block should keep his feet moving as in pass blocking action, driving the defensive man back. This blocking action has the added advantage of keeping the linebacker from scraping off to the inside and making the tackle, or making the back run out of his running lane.

If the defensive end turns into the motion man, who is using pass block action against him, it becomes easier for the tight end to drive him upfield. This is because the end has no leverage or leg power to keep his momentum going. The defensive player cannot turn his back if the blocker keeps him faced off with the pass block action. As mentioned earlier, this blocking action also keeps the defensive end from being clipped.

The tight end must be cautioned not to lunge out at his man. He should come up in pass blocking position, feet moving, shoulders parallel to the line of scrimmage—and must stay with his man. The face off must be maintained so that the defensive end doesn't penetrate.

The proper timing and blocking procedure can be mastered fairly quickly in drill time. Have a player with an air dummy simulate the defensive end. A three back and tight end can be used, or fullback and tight end, or the whole backfield and tight end. See Diagram 7-16.

When the fullback motion is used, yet another advantage emerges in that the halfback dive option opens up (Diagram 7-17).

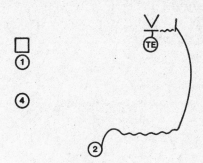

Diagram 7-16

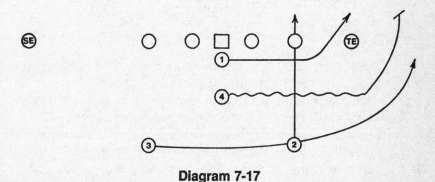

Diagram 7-17

SCOOP BLOCKING ON THE WEDGE BLOCK

Wedge blocking is generally used for short yardage situations, or inside the 10 yard line. It is an important part of line blocking for the Pro-Bone.

A problem arises in that, when regular splits are used, a linebacker can sometimes beat the lineman into the gap and thus break up the effectiveness of the wedge block. Another problem can be the "tailgating" of the lineman coming down to form the wedge—not getting a good seal on the wedge formation.

Before describing our solution to these problems, we should mention an additional situation for which we think wedge blocking is particularly effective. This is when the defense is giving an eight-man front look by blitzing linebackers or stunting in the line. Against this, the wedge block by the line provides better protection for the back, plus allowing a better chance for him to break loose into the secondary.

To return to the problem areas above, one sees that in the normal wedge block the linemen usually come straight to the lead blocker to form the wedge, as in Diagram 7-18.

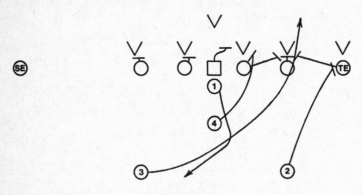

Diagram 7-18

The momentum of the linemen is toward the lead blocker and not upfield. By changing to what can be called a "scoop block," the momentum can be changed from inward motion to upfield motion. This also seems to form a better pocket with more force.

Below are the specific changes required; we will use Wedge 36 to demonstrate. The wedge will be shown from regular splits.

The right guard pulls, using the elbow-to-the-side pulling technique, the same as the one used for the end sweep. When the guard reaches the lead blocking tackle, he steps with the right foot, executes a turn upfield block, and turns in to the shoulder of the lead blocker. The guard forces his right shoulder into the back of the shoulder of the lead blocker. See Diagram 7-19. When the right shoulder makes contact, the head should turn slightly outward to keep the force of his weight going upfield.

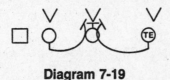

Diagram 7-19

The lead blocker will shield block, which means he will come across low and hard on all fours, forcing his head up into the crotch of the defensive man, sliding the helmet up to waist high if possible.

The tight end pulls to the left, using the same technique as the guard, but making contact with the left shoulder and stepping up into the lead man off the left foot.

The two back runs a curve pattern, making contact with the defensive man waist-high. He blocks from the outside of the man across to the inside hip, then turns his helmet to the outside. This forces the defensive man outside. (Diagram 7-20.)

If the defensive man is squared off, the halfback must block straight into him, moving the head to the outside hip and then forcing the defensive man to the outside.

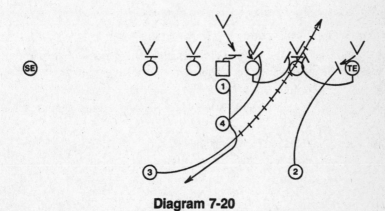

Diagram 7-20

The fullback uses the same technique as the two back, getting to the blocking area as quickly as possible, blocking through the man and turning him outside. All of this enables the three back to cheat in and up and hit the hole more quickly. The rest of the line blocks down in gaps to cover, so the three back doesn't get hit before he gets to the hole.

We will conclude our "nuts and bolts" chapter with discussions of timing for the passing game, ball control, cadence, and the huddle.

TIMING OF THE PASSING GAME

A good passing game doesn't just happen. Hard work is required to get the odds in favor of pass completions and to diminish the fear of using the pass as a key part of your total offense.

While they may seem obvious, the keys to a successful pass offense are these: 1) The QB knows where the receiver is going to be when he throws the ball. 2) The receiver goes to the proper areas of his different pass routes. 3) The QB sets up at the proper distance for each pattern.

The crucial factor is timing. Timing of the patterns must be learned so thoroughly that looking for the ball at the proper time becomes automatic.

These procedures should raise completion rates:

1. Time receivers individually, so that each knows the distance he must cover in a given pattern and how long it will take to cover it.

2. Time the QB on his set-up distance.

3. Time each pattern.

4. Have the QB throw while being blitzed, recording the time when he would be sacked. This is an aid for learning to go to the flare back or short receiver.

5. Time pass patterns when the offense is going against a live secondary.

6. The receiving coach should work the QB on throwing to receivers when they become open on cuts. This means that the QB must learn to throw on the cut, just before the receiver comes open.

7. Time pass patterns from snap to QB release to reception.

8. Time sets of plays: options, sweeps, counters, quick pitches and reverses.

9. Stretching drills should be done before and after practice.

10. Use overload workouts to teach and show players how pain barriers can be overcome.

11. Run sprints of 10, 20, 30, and 40 yards, using these distances in timed drills.

BALL CONTROL

Ball control in a game means more than 3 or 4 yards and a cloud of dust. Running the ball well does control a game, but there are some small, additional things you can do that aid greatly in controlling the clock.

Ball control also relates to the two-minute offense, and being able to come back into a ball game without losing poise.

These procedures should help control games:

1. Time huddles. The QB has to know how long a 25-second huddle is, to avoid being called for delay of game, and to be able to use as much time as possible when that is to the offense's advantage. This can be learned by timing huddles in practice. Plays can be repeated until the timing is mastered.

2. The quick huddle can be used to advantage when time is a factor in a scoring drive. A stopwatch can be used in practice, and players should make the huddle-to-snap time 12 seconds. The team should run the play correctly, then sprint back to the huddle, calling the play without hesitation. They should be required to run six correct plays in the allotted time before being allowed to quit.

3. Have the QB call the play on the line of scrimmage without a huddle. Again, six perfect plays should be run before quitting.

4. Teach receivers to stay in bounds when running down the clock.

CADENCE

In addition to effective play selection, incorporating the blocking techniques just discussed, defenses—especially changing defenses—can be further confused by variations in cadence.

Regular Cadence

Here is the regular cadence procedure:

1. The word "set" is used to make sure that the team is set, ready to go on either a quick count or silent count (which would start on the word "set").

2. Color permits the use of audibles on the line of scrimmage. A hot color is used during the practice week. Should the quarterback wish to change a play on the line of scrimmage, he uses the hot color. If the hot color is not used, then the next play has no meaning.

3. The next sound after the color is the number of the play (see play numbers in earlier chapters), such as 22. If the hot color is used, 22 would be Option Right and would replace the play called in the huddle. The automatics usually come on the second count, although this is not a hard and fast rule. If the defense starts to realize that the ball is being snapped on the second count, it should be changed.

4. The next sound is "hit one—hit two—hit three." The ball goes on the "hit" sound. This gets the line off the line of scrimmage with the ball, as the center hikes at the sound of "hit."

Silent Count

If defenses start to get used to a certain cadence, and they begin to get the jump on offensive linemen, the silent count can be used. Defenses tend to jump offside when the silent count is used. It should be even more useful with the new rule that forbids defensive players from breaking the plane of the line of scrimmage. This is how it works:

1. The quarterback begins with the regular cadence: "set," a color, a play, then "hit one, hit two," etc.

2. When using the silent count, the quarterback simply says "set." Hearing this, the team starts counting "one thousand one, one thousand two," etc., to themselves.

3. The quarterback will have said in the huddle, "Second two, count silent count." When he is sure the team is positioned, he says "Set." The other players, to themselves, then count "one thousand one, one thousand two," and the ball is hiked on the

"thousand" before the "two." The defense doesn't know when the ball will be moving.

4. The silent count can be practiced in the locker room, at team meetings and before the game. The quarterback will say, "Silent count, third number." He then calls, "Set," and the team says out loud, together, "One thousand one, one thousand two, one thousand three." At the thousand before the three, the players clap their hands together. It is easy to pick up any players having difficulty with the count. Five minutes practice time per day is usually enough for silent count.

It is easy, while the team is dressing, to have the quarterback call out cadence and have the team clap or shout "go" on the correct count. This helps minimize offside calls during games, and helps bring the team together in terms of thinking about cadence. As a coach, you know that getting off the ball aggressively is crucial. Time spent on cadence is never wasted time.

Broken Cadence

Along with regular cadence and silent count, a broken cadence can also be used. This further complicates things for defenses. They have to adjust to different splits, different spacings—and now different cadences. The broken cadence is used like this:

1. When the team is positioned, the quarterback calls the regular "set." He then pauses. The defense must now wait for a silent count or start an adjustment in their alignment.

2. After the pause, the quarterback will say the color, the play, pause, then "hit one, hit two," pause, "hit three." He can pause at any point in the cadence count he wishes.

3. The quarterback will have told the team in the huddle that it will be broken cadence, third count.

Considering the variety possible in the cadence count, we should stress again the value of a comfortable starting stance and good eye contact with the defense. Also remember the 5-minute practice period on cadence to instill the proper mental attitude (and to stay onside). A further variation is the quick count, going on "set." The quick count can be used to advantage on passing and quick plays, keeping the defense from moving around and getting the jump on the ball.

THE HUDDLE

The huddle is formed 8 yards from the ball. The center forms the huddle. Diagram 7-21 shows how it is organized.

The quarterback steps into the huddle and gives the play. He does not mention split if it is regular. If it is to be a wide or short split, the quarterback says so, as in "split wide, second count."

The split end and center go to the line of scrimmage. The quarterback repeats the play and the count, then says "Break." The remaining players clap their hands, say "Break," and run to the line of scrimmage.

On the line of scrimmage, the quarterback will look at the defensive alignment and check to see that the offense is set. He then says "Set," color, play, then "Hit one, hit two."

You should time the huddles and remind the players that consistency of huddle time is important.

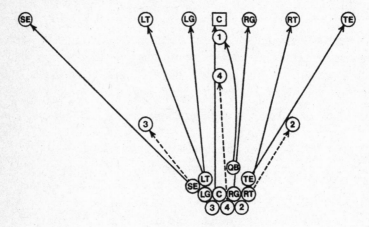

Diagram 7-21

8

Drills for the
Pro-Bone

Drill time is time spent in putting coaching theory into practice. An enjoyable aspect of football at any level is seeing coaching ideas being put into action. Although it seems obvious that they should, some coaches don't spend practice time on drills that complement their offenses. Drill time should be organized to develop the specific skills required for a given offense.

Pre-season is the time for careful selection of drills. The use of a chart that lists skills and features to be stressed on both offense and defense should be a priority. Weekly practices should be charted, and you should record the time spent in such drills as blocking, ball handling, pass receiving, passing, guards pulling, pass blocking, and center snaps.

Early in the week, decide on a game strategy and select drills to complement that strategy. After the game, the charts can be reexamined to determine whether weaknesses apparent during the game can be traced to inadequate preparation. During games, you should have someone scout your own team for weaknesses.

Diagram 8-1 shows a sample chart that could be used to keep track of drill time. You will probably add or subtract items from the list to suit your own purposes.

Sample Drill Chart

	First Week						Second Week						Third Week					
Conditioning																		
Lectures																		
Chalk talks																		
QB sessions																		
Staff meetings																		
Pre-game drill																		
Signal drill																		
Skeleton drill																		
Dummy scrimmage																		
Actual scrimmage																		
Cadence drill																		
Shoulder block																		
Cross block																		
Wedge block																		
Punt block																		
Downfield block																		
Skeleton backs																		
Two-on-one drill																		
Three-on-one drill																		
Punt																		
Kickoff																		
Guards pulling																		
Pass blocking																		
Quickness drills																		
Silent count																		
FB reading drills																		
Pass drills																		
50																		
60																		
70																		
90																		
Two-minute offense																		
10-yard offense																		
Goal line defense																		
Extra points																		
Field goals																		
Stretching exercise																		
Receiving drills																		
Linebacker drills																		
Cornerback drills																		
Turnout time																		

Diagram 8-1

Here now are specific drills related to the Pro-Bone.

HANDOFF DRILL

The purpose of this drill is to coordinate the depth and timing of the halfbacks with the fullback on the option play.

1. Line up the backfield with the halfbacks 4½ yards deep and the fullback 2 feet behind the QB.
2. Mark off the line on a fire hose or put dummies 8 feet from the center. The 8 feet is tackle distance from the center.
3. Chalk in lines 1½ feet in back of the tackle area for the area where the halfback and the quarterback will engage.
4. A coach stands about 6 feet away and tells the backfield option left or option right. The coach can grade or provide assistance to the QB from this position.
5. Position the second backfield behind the first, ready to come forward and run the option. (See Diagram 8-2.)

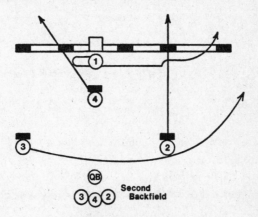

Diagram 8-2

SPACING DRILL

The objectives of this drill are twofold: First, it helps the halfbacks line up properly on short, regular and wide splits. Second, it helps the QB learn how to read whether or not the halfback is open for the handoff.

1. The drill uses a full backfield, a center and two tackles.
2. Huddle the backfield, center and tackles. The QB calls the split and option right or left.

3. On the QB break signal, the skeleton team comes up to the fire hose for the running of the play.

4. The QB runs the option, faking to the FB and coming down the line of scrimmage to read the block of the tackle. If the dummy is driven off the line of scrimmage, the QB hands off. If not, the QB keeps and continues the option.

5. Standing dummies are used for the tackles to block against. (See Diagram 8-3.)

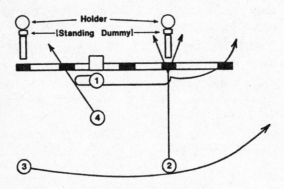

Diagram 8-3

HALFBACK READS AND ROUTES

The object of this drill is to teach reads on the option play. The drill is done without tackles.

1. Line up two standup dummies over the hole that the FB would go through, two dummies over the tackle hole, and position one man with an air dummy as a defensive end.

2. Instruct the dummy holders on which hole to leave open, and check to see if the QB makes the right choice.

3. The QB brings the backfield to the line and runs the play.

4. The players holding the dummies place the bottoms of the dummies together, forming a V.

5. The players holding the dummies either bring them together or leave them apart.

6. The DE with the air dummy says "one thousand one, one thousand two," then comes toward the QB to play the option.

7. The QB should hand off to the back where the V is—where the dummies are left open. If all the dummies are closed he should pitch to the trailing back. (Diagram 8-4.)

8. Have other backfields waiting to run the play.

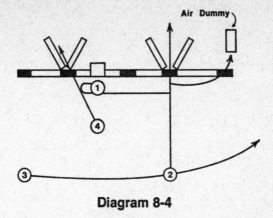

Air Dummy

Diagram 8-4

TEAM DRILL

The purpose of this drill is to provide practice on all parts of the option.

1. Line up as many as four backfields with centers.
2. Set dummies on four corners, 20 yards apart.
3. Station one coach in the middle or two coaches diagonally in the square to watch and grade each unit.
4. Station 1: option handoff to FB. Station 2: handoff to HB. Station 3: QB keeper. Station 4: pitch to trailing HB. (See Diagram 8-5.)

SILENT COUNT

This drill teaches silent count and cadence.

1. Have a defensive unit, using dummies, set up the defensive alignments that will be faced in a given week.
2. Huddle the offensive team and have the QB give the cadence, silent count, third number.
3. Have the QB say the set-color-number. As soon as the number is said, the team counts out loud together, "one thousand one, one thousand two," and all clap together on the three.
4. The QB then gives the count in the huddle. The team breaks to the line of scrimmage and runs the play on the silent count.
5. The QB can give any starting number—first, second, third or fourth count. The team always claps together for the last number. If a two count is given, it is "one thousand one, one thousand *clap*," together.

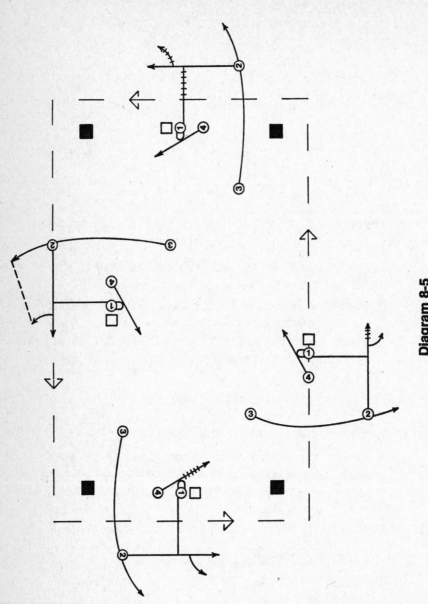

Diagram 8-5

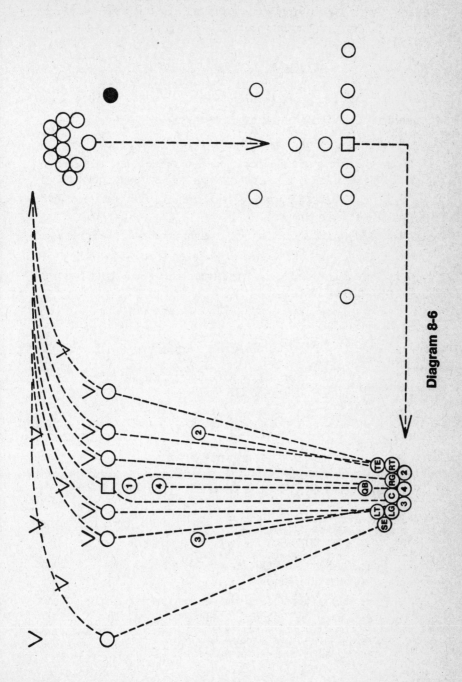

Diagram 8-6

6. Station another coach to the side of the dummies (Diagram 8-6), and have the team run over to him and run a play on regular count, then return to the dummy area to run another play.

FULLBACK READING DRILL

The purpose of this drill is to help the FB cut to the proper running lane by reading the block of the guard.

1. The drill requires the QB, center, two guards, and the FB.
2. The defense plays over the guards or inside them, or off the line of scrimmage. The defensive men should use air dummies.
3. The QB calls the play in a short huddle and brings the team to the line of scrimmage.
4. The offense should run five to eight minutes of live scrimmage.
5. The FB cuts off the block to daylight. (See Diagram 8-7.)
6. The guards should practice drive, drive reverse cut-off, and cut-off blocks.

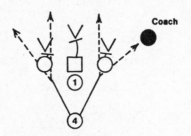

Diagram 8-7

LINEMEN BLOCKING AND POSITIONING DRILL

The object of this drill is to teach linemen short, regular and wide splits, plus provide work on wedge blocking.

1. The drill requires QB and regular offensive line—two tackles, two guards, center and TE.
2. Set up a dummy defense and have the QB call different offensive sets, using the different line adjustments.
3. A coach stands behind defense to grade offense and watch for correct alignment. (Diagram 8-8.)

Diagram 8-8

PASS DRILLS FOR 50, 60, 70 AND 90 SERIES

This drill helps pass receivers learn patterns.

1. Use two backfields, TE and SE.
2. A coach stands between the units and calls the patterns he wants. (See Diagram 8-9.)
3. One team huddles and one team runs the desired pattern.
4. When one team has run a pattern, the other breaks to the line of scrimmage to run their pattern.
5. Alternating groups keeps all players working.

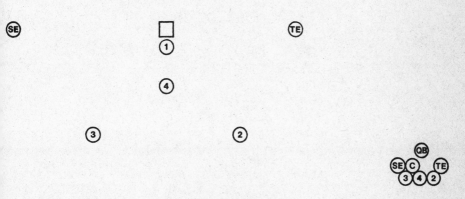

Diagram 8-9

RECEIVING DRILL

This drill is designed to help receivers concentrate on watching the ball into their hands.

1. Use two lines—one of split ends, one of tight ends.

2. Use two coaches, or one coach and a QB to throw the ball.
3. Have everyone in each line
    a) catch a quick look in.
    b) run 5 yards and make catch with left hand.
    c) run 5 yards and make catch with right hand.
    d) catch a ball thrown low at the ankles.
    e) catch a lob pass over the head.
    f) tip a pass three times before catching it.
    g) get hit with an air dummy as the catch is made. (See Diagram 8-10.)

Diagram 8-10

NON-CONTACT DRILL

The purpose of this drill is to help the team run automatic calls from the line of scrimmage.

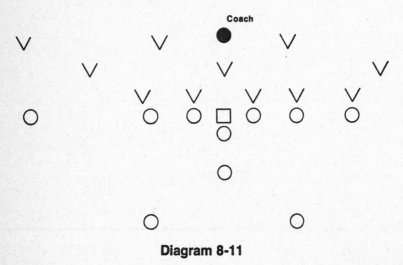

Diagram 8-11

1. This drill can be run without a dummy defense.

2. Full offensive team lines up (dummy defense can be used if so desired).

3. A coach calls one of five plays that has been agreed upon for the coming game.

4. QB calls signals and runs the play immediately after the coach has named the play.

5. The coach grades the offensive team on execution. (Diagram 8-11.)

6. The coach can set points for plays run correctly, and work the team until the required number of points is achieved.

PASS PROTECTION

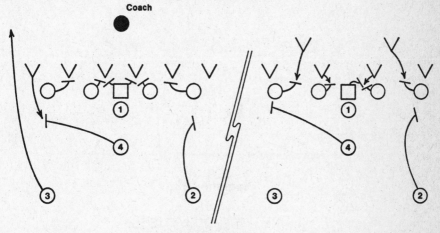

Diagram 8-12

In this drill, linemen and blocking backs are helped to keep defensive flow to the outside.

1. Line up a seven-man gap front or a 5-2, 4-4 stack defense.

2. Blitz everyone on each play. Have the defensive players use dummies.

3. Have the linemen block inside seam, with the HB and FB blocking the first outside defensive men. (See Diagram 8-12.)

4. Have the QB step up into the pocket so the defense will flow outside.

WEDGE BLOCKING DRILL

The object of this drill is for the linemen to form a wedge, keeping tight to the center man so that defensive players are forced outside.

1. Line up defensive players over offensive players or in the gaps, depending on the coach's call.
2. The QB calls the play in the huddle or on the line of scrimmage.
3. When wedge blocking, have linemen put head and shoulder tight into the lead blocker to prevent penetration by the defense.
4. Use large, standup dummies if possible. (Diagram 8-13.)

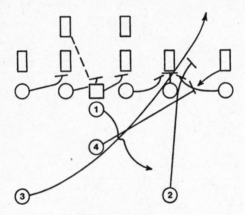

Diagram 8-13

IMPROVING QUICKNESS

It is rather difficult to talk about quickness because it is, in part, a God-given talent. It can be improved, however. To improve both team and individual quickness, the following points should prove helpful in keeping players alert to the quickness concept.

1. Practice sessions should always be run to a schedule and drills should be kept on time.
2. Players should sprint from one drill area to another.
3. Players and the team should be rewarded for practices in which their effort is 100 percent.
4. Sprints are timed by stopwatch, and all players are to know and try to improve their times.

5. Off season preparation should include running and stretching exercises.

6. The track coach should be brought in five or six times during the season to work on improving times.

7. The team should be timed on how fast they can run six correct plays from the huddle to the line of scrimmage.

THE TWO-MINUTE OFFENSE

We turn now to drills for the two-minute offense. Before getting to the drills themselves, the following considerations affecting the two-minute offense should be discussed:

1. The kind of score needed, whether 8, 7, or 3 points.

2. Field position.

3. The type of defense being used.

4. The strengths of your offense.

5. Whether your team can call plays effectively from the line of scrimmage.

6. The number of timeouts remaining.

In addition, if a team is to run the two-minute offense successfully, the following need special attention:

1. Bench to field communication.

2. Identification of special players needed for this offense.

3. Proper organization of the bench—to get this team on the field when needed.

4. Organization of the two-minute offense itself, so that players are confident running it.

5. Quarterback knowledge of plays to be run (especially the first one), so that valuable time is not wasted.

These factors must be incorporated into the game plan, with coaches being assigned specific areas of responsibility. You could appoint a special teams coach, for example, who would be responsible for knowing which players are to be substituted in specific situations. The head coach could check down, time, and field position change. A spotter above could check any defensive change or defensive weaknesses that could be taken advantage of by the offense.

TWO-MINUTE OFFENSE DRILL

The purpose of this drill is to teach the use of field and the proper use of time for quick scoring.

1. This is a good drill for light days, Thursdays and Mondays.
2. Use full field, and have a coach present the time and situation to the QB.
3. Ahead of time, the coach should set up a three-play sequence or out-of-bounds play for the QB to run.
4. The coach calls out the three-play sequence.
5. QB calls three plays in huddle, then runs plays without huddling again.
6. QB changes a play on the line of scrimmage if it is inappropriate to the situation.
7. One coach keeps the ball ready for play. Another coach can grade players on execution.

THE 10-YARD OFFENSE

The object of this drill is to teach proper play selection within the 10 yard line.

1. Use full team offense and full team defense.
2. Have either live scrimmage, or let the defense use air dummies.
3. If the defense uses air dummies, the ball is down where the man with the dummy hits the runner.
4. Score live scrimmage on points, three points to the defense if they stop the offense in four plays.
5. Give two points to the offense for a TD, one point for point after or field goal.
6. Use a quick whistle.
7. Make sure offensive line splits are cut down.

FULLBACK BLOCKING DRILL

This drill teaches the fullback how to block defensive ends.

1. The drill requires dummy holders to be defensive ends.

2. The dummy holders can use three positions: a) come across the line of scrimmage and box to the inside, b) slant hard to the inside, or c) float on the line of scrimmage.

3. The fullback will line up in his regular stance and, on the coach's signal, he will go down the line of scrimmage (Diagram 8-14) and block the defensive end.

4. The fullback should use the following kinds of blocks: a) The straight ahead shoulder block, driving through the defensive end. b) The fullback comes hard toward the end, aiming for a high shoulder block, then at the last minute puts his shoulder down and blocks through the lower legs. Once contact is made, he drives through the defensive player with a crab block. c) The fullback comes hard toward the end low, then at the last minute comes up hard with his shoulder, blocking through the end's chest and shoulder area.

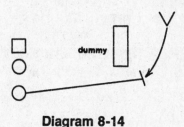

Diagram 8-14

BLOCK DOWN, SHORT TRAP DRILL

With this drill, linemen are taught to block gap defenders and trap.

1. This is a full line drill in which the line works together.

2. The line huddles and comes to the line of scrimmage. The defenders hold hand dummies and go to the offensive gaps. (Diagram 8-15.)

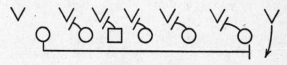

Diagram 8-15

3. The weakside tackle comes down the line of scrimmage and blocks the first man to the outside.

4. The offensive linemen block down to the gaps with shoulder blocks, going to reverse cut-off blocks.

5. If the trap is a man inside the 6 hole, the first outside lineman blocks the first defensive man on his outside shoulder. (See Diagram 8-16.)

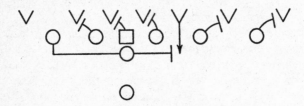

Diagram 8-16

OPTION BLOCKING DRILL FOR OFFENSIVE TACKLES

This drill presents different blocking situations for the offensive tackles, so that there is no hesitation when blocking for the option. (See Diagram 8-17.)

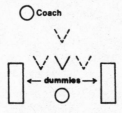

Diagram 8-17

1. The offensive tackle turns his back to a coach and the defensive player.

2. The coach tells the defensive player which position to assume.

3. The coach blows the whistle and the tackle turns to face him. The coach holds up the number of fingers for the starting count that the tackle will go on.

4. The coach says "set." The tackle gets into his stance, the coach counts the cadence, and the tackle performs his block.

5. The blocks that can be used are: a) straight on block, b) straight on, reverse crab block, c) outside knee cut-off block, d) block

down gap technique, e) scoop block, and f) come high, low leg
block.

DOWNFIELD BLOCKING DRILL FOR LINEMEN

The purposes of this drill are to teach linemen, first, to block
on the line of scrimmage, and second, to block well downfield. A
good blocking base is taught by using a board to keep the linemen's
feet apart. (See Diagram 8-18.)

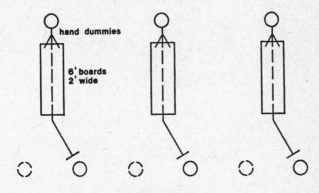

Diagram 8-18

1. The offensive lineman drives a defensive player with a hand
   dummy down the length of the board.
2. At the end of the board, the lineman sprints downfield and blocks
   another player holding a hand dummy.
3. Linemen should use: a) high low block, b) cut-off block, and c)
   hit and drive through block.
4. The downfield dummy holder should move to the side opposite
   the lineman he has been blocking, so that the lineman learns to
   block to either side downfield.

FULLBACK BLOCKING GAP DEFENSE DRILL

This drill coordinates the fullback's trap blocking with that of
the offensive line when blocking a gap defense.

1. The drill requires the offensive line, the fullback, and defensive
   players holding hand dummies.

2. The line blocks down to the gaps, with the fullback blocking the first defensive player loose outside. (Diagram 8-19.)

3. If the fullback short traps inside the first man outside the trap area, he blocks the first man outside. (Diagram 8-20.)

4. Have the fullback practice blocking all holes, with the linemen outside the holes blocking out. (See Diagram 8-21.)

5. The offensive linemen huddle, and when the quarterback or coach calls the hole to be trapped, they come to the line of scrimmage, and run the play.

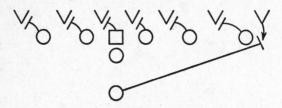

Diagram 8-19

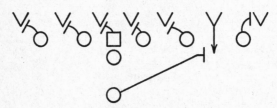

Diagram 8-20

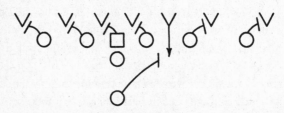

Diagram 8-21

END COMING OFF THE LINE DRILL

This drill is designed to teach receivers to run their pass routes after they've been hit on the line of scrimmage.

1. Receivers line up in a straight line. A quarterback or coach throws the ball.

2. A defensive end lines up opposite the offensive player and either a) hits the receiver as he comes off the line of scrimmage, b) cuts the receiver, c) pushes to the outside, or d) bumps and runs. (See Diagram 8-22.)

3. The receiver should a) jab step, b) roll off the defensive man, c) adjust his split, d) forward roll, e) move upfield, parallel to the line of scrimmage, outside, or f) hit the defensive man and roll off.

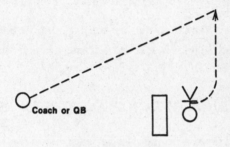

Diagram 8-22

RECEIVERS' FUMBLE PREVENTION DRILL

The purpose of this drill is to improve receivers' concentration and minimize fumbling.

1. A coach or quarterback throws to receivers. (Diagram 8-23.)

2. Two players with air dummies hit the receivers as they catch the ball.

3. Receivers run through dummies after catching the ball.

4. Two more dummy holders can be added, increasing resistance.

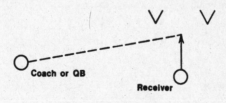

Diagram 8-23

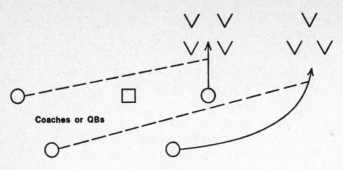

Diagram 8-24

5. Receivers should run the 50 series against the dummies.

6. Dummies should be set in the same manner and hit halfbacks flaring out of the backfield. (Diagram 8-24.)

FULLBACK OPTION DOUBLE-TEAM DRILL

This drill focuses on the double-team block used when an odd defense is utilized against the option.

1. Either half or all of the offensive line can be used, along with the fullback and quarterback.

2. Defensive players holding hand dummies line up in an odd front, as in Diagram 8-25.

3. Offensive tackles always come across in front of the defensive tackles and block the inside linebackers.

4. The line and fullback huddle. The quarterback gives the play, breaks to the line of scrimmage, and the play is run.

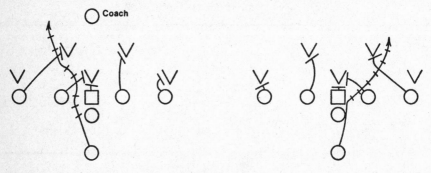

Diagram 8-25

5. The linemen can line up without a huddle. With the quarterback calling plays on the line of scrimmage, see how many can be run correctly in three minutes.

POWER 36 DOUBLE-TEAM DRILL

This drill concentrates on double-team blocking between the tight end, split end, and tackle. It also teaches the ends how to slide-off block the linebacker.

1. Two sets of offensive tackles are required, along with a tight end or split end.
2. Line up the defensive tackles on, in the seam, or slanting down. Add two inside linebackers. (See Diagram 8-26.)

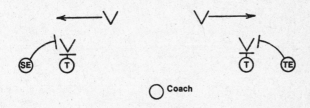

Diagram 8-26

3. A coach stands behind the offensive players and tells the defense in which direction they are to go.
4. The offense turns around and gets the count.
5. When the defense slants down, the ends scrape-off block on the defensive player and block the linebacker inside. (Diagram 8-27.)

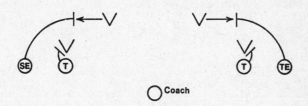

Diagram 8-27

GUARD PULLING DRILL

This drill teaches guards proper pulling techniques and how to seal block inside when cutting upfield. (See Diagram 8-28.)

1. From a three-point stance, the guard pulls on the quarterback's count down the line of scrimmage, using the technique described in Chapter 7.

2. The guard should be timed to see how long it takes to get to the blocking area.

3. The guard should be taught to make his pull under control, using his outside foot to make a clean cut upfield, filling to the inside.

4. The following blocks can be used: a) cut block, b) high low, c) low high block, and d) reverse cut-off block.

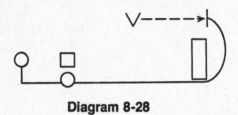

Diagram 8-28

DOUBLE-TEAM PULL THROUGH DRILL

This drill teaches double-team blocking, using the backs and line together. It improves the timing and blocking of the guard's short pull and block on the linebacker.

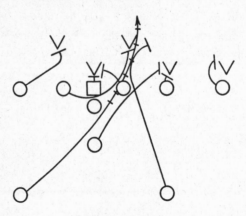

Diagram 8-29

1. The full line and backs are used in dummy scrimmage. (Diagram 8-29.)

2. The defense should use air dummies and be aggressive.

3. Have the center and guard, tackle and fullback, work together on the double-team. (Diagram 8-30.)

4. Offensive players should use the high low double-team. The man over the defensive player should force him straight back using a crab block. The guard and fullback seal block.

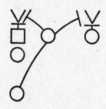

Diagram 8-30

200-YARD OFFENSIVE TEAM DRILL

This drill emphasizes running plays from the line of scrimmage. Early in the season, it is a good conditioning drill as well. Coaches grade each play as it is run.

1. The offensive team lines up on the goal line and runs half passing plays, half running plays every 10 yards down to the opposite goal line and back.

2. A coach follows with clip board, timing and grading each play.

3. Plays are to cover only 10 yards. On pass plays, the receiver brings the ball back to the appropriate yard line.

The drills outlined in this chapter should help to accomplish the following:

1. All drills facilitate the running of the Pro-Bone.

2. Most stress the time factor—short drills cover each area of the offense.

3. Players' motivation and enthusiasm can be heightened through running drills that take 10 to 15 minutes, at 110 percent.

4. Goals are accomplished with a minimum of contact.

5. Drills can be used to polish weak areas, as scouting reports or statistics indicate.

6. Posted drill charts increase efficiency, since the players know what is to be worked on in a given practice.

9

Effective Pro-Bone
Play Selection
for Specific Defenses

Now that familiarity with the Pro-Bone has been established, we would like to get more specific and show how the offense can be most effectively used against a variety of defenses.

A chart detailing the defense an opponent will use is a good starting point in planning drill time and offensive strategy. Most defenses today employ zone coverage, so part of the chart should include open areas and weaknesses of the particular zone to be encountered. This information should be on game cards so that it can be readily available during the game.

Deciding on drills and plays for a specific opponent involves consideration of your own personnel. From the group of plays appropriate for a given opponent, the offensive coach should choose those that take full advantage of, say, a great right tackle, a strong trapping guard, or a quick split end.

The play selections in this chapter should be run to the weakness of the given defense. Furthermore, plans should be made to run toward the opponent's weaker players, who are revealed in scouting charts.

Once plays have been selected and a total game plan formulated, it's probably best to stay with them during the actual game. The week's practice has been devoted to those plays and concepts, so the percentages would seem to favor the prepared areas. The players should retain more confidence, and the coaches will be able to see where errors are being made and make the necessary adjustments.

Diagrams in this chapter include:

1. Boxed areas, which indicate areas of weakness in a given defense.

2. A list of running plays that should work against that defense.

3. Pass patterns that should be run to the weakness of the secondary.

The 4-3 Defense (Diagram 9-1)

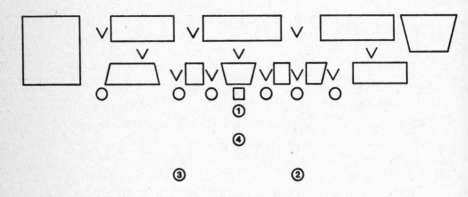

Diagram 9-1

Running offense

1. Power 36-25.
2. Quick Pitch 28 and 37.
3. Lead Options 21-32 (could use wedge blocking).
4. Lead Option Right and Left (use the fullback).
5. Quarterback Power Rollouts Right and Left.
6. Quick Pitch 37, Fullback Trap 23.
7. Crossbuck 34-23.
8. Tackle Trap 13-14, Quarterback Carries.

Passing offense

1. Patterns 91-93.
2. Patterns 70-72.
3. Pattern 81.

4. Patterns 60-62.

5. Quick Series 51-57.

6. Quick Pitch, Halfback Pass Left and Right.

7. Lead Option Pass Right and Left.

8. Power 36-25, Halfback Pass.

The 4-3 Defense can be attacked readily to the outside, because the Pro 4-3 was designed to cover halfbacks set closer to the line of scrimmage than they are in the Pro-Bone. Furthermore, the offense has good angle advantages and is not outnumbered at the line of scrimmage.

Diagram 9-2 shows point of attack blocking for the running plays, Power 36 or 25. Diagram 9-3 illustrates the 25 Inside or Double TE, and Quick Pitches are shown in Diagram 9-4.

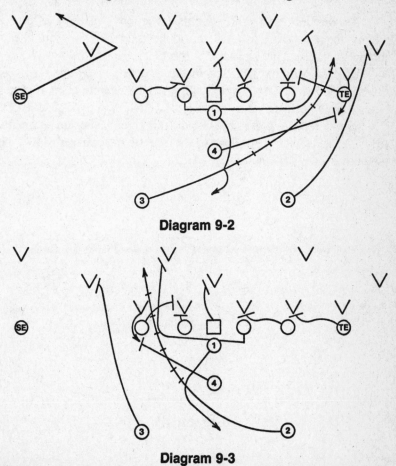

Diagram 9-2

Diagram 9-3

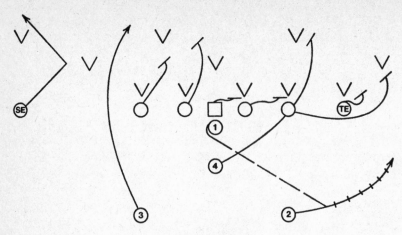

Diagram 9-4

As we said, this kind of outside action is usually effective against the 4-3. Traps and crossbucks keep the defense from cheating and cut defensive flow.

Blocking for the fullback in the middle can be changed. As Diagram 9-5 shows, the center and guard can double team to either side, with the offside tackle slanting down to pick up the linebacker.

The defensive tackle has a hard time coming inside to hit the fullback, since being so close to the line of scrimmage allows the latter to hit the hole quickly.

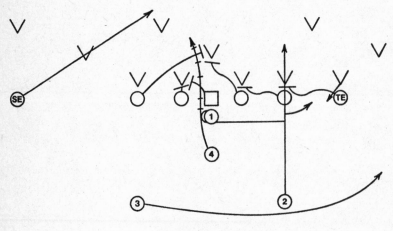

Diagram 9-5

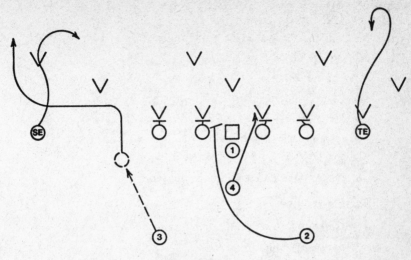

Diagram 9-6

The 70 series exploits the 4-3 on the outside zone. Diagram 9-6 shows the 4-3 coverage on the 72 Crossbuck Pass.

The outside corner must cover flat and the defensive half the split end, man-to-man—in other words, one-on-one coverage.

The 60 series also provides good outside routes, making the defense adjust to three men in a zone.

5-2 Monster Three Deep (Diagram 9-7)

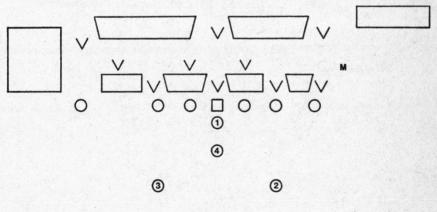

Diagram 9-7

Running offense

1. Option Left and Right, using fullback.
2. Sweep 27-29.
3. 325 Reverse.
4. 23 Crossbuck.
5. Lead Options Left, 21-23, and 32 Lead Right.
6. Quarterback Power Rollout Left.
7. Trap 23.
8. Quick Pitch Left with Fullback Trap.

Passing offense

1. Pattern 92.
2. Pattern 81 Left.
3. 70 Left, Flea-Flicker 72.
4. 60 Left, 62 Left.
5. 50-54-57.
6. Stand Up and Go.
7. Quick Pitch Left, Halfback Pass.
8. Quarterback Power Rollout Right and Left Pass.
9. Power 36 Halfback Pass.
10. Lead Option Right Pass.

The 5-2 Monster can also be attacked effectively with the Pro-Bone, because the offense's balanced backfield allows more

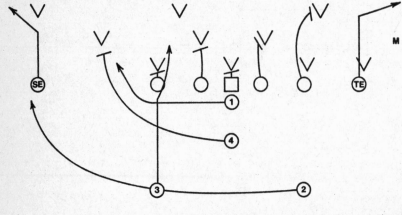

Diagram 9-8

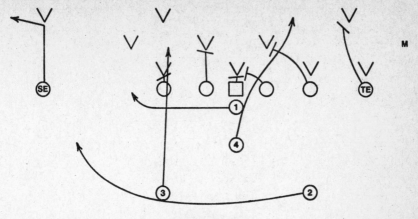

Diagram 9-9

offensive than defensive players in the defensive area. An example is shown in Diagram 9-8 for the Lead Option Left.

The Pro-Bone also attacks the middle of the 5-2 successfully with the fullback. Diagram 9-9 illustrates (Option Left), showing the guard double team, slant down tackle.

The counter action of the fullback makes the monster stay home and cuts down the angle of pursuit. This is due to the fact that the fullback can get into the secondary so quickly.

Using the Fake Option Right and throwing to the split end on a short flag pattern keeps the defensive half from coming up and supporting on the option play.

Throwing the halfback pass is an additional way to keep pressure on the defensive half and monster. The latter usually plays close to the line of scrimmage against the Pro-Bone, respecting the run.

The key to halfback passing is to work on it during the off season. Most halfbacks will welcome the opportunity to do something different. They needn't be great passers, but they do have to make the passing plays look like running plays, and then get the ball away. The pass off the fake option is usually lofted, and not difficult to throw.

5-2 Oklahoma (Diagram 9-10)

Running offense

1. Option Left and Right, QB Keep or Pitch (use fullback).
2. 21-32 Lead (can wedge block).

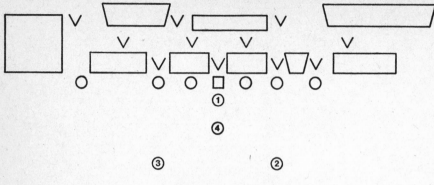

Diagram 9-10

3. QB Power Rollouts Left and Right.

4. Wide Sweeps 38-29.

5. Crossbuck 23-34.

6. 325-326 Reverses.

7. Tackle Trap 13.

(Split line to wide set.)

Passing offense

1. Pattern 93.

2. 81 Left and Right.

3. Pattern 70 Left and Right.

4. Patterns 60-61-62 (individual crossing patterns off motion).

5. Power 27-38 Motion, Halfback Pass.

6. Regular Option Right and Left, TE Deep.

Attacking the 5-2 Okie is about the same as attacking the 5-2 Monster, except that running to the strong side is more successful due to the absence of the monster.

Combining the double-team option inside with the power sweeps gives good blocking advantages. The 5-2 is basically set up for the option and not power. As Diagram 9-11 shows for the 32 Lead, inside leads are particularly effective.

Power leads can open up fake power leads, off which the quarterback can throw to the tight end or split end. This type of action again keeps the defensive halfback from coming up to support. See Diagram 9-12 for the 32 Lead Pass to TE.

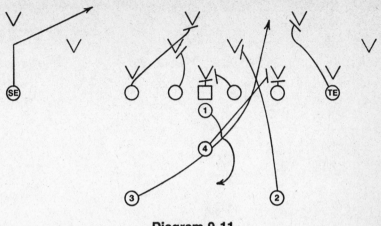

Diagram 9-11

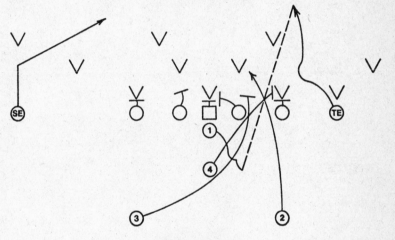

Diagram 9-12

5-3 Defense (Diagram 9-13)

Running offense

(Wide split in line.)

1. Option Left and Right, QB Keep and Pitch to HB.
2. Quick Pitch 37-28.
3. Lead 32-21 (wedge blocking).
4. Trap 34-23.
5. Power 36 and 25.
6. Crossbuck 34-23.

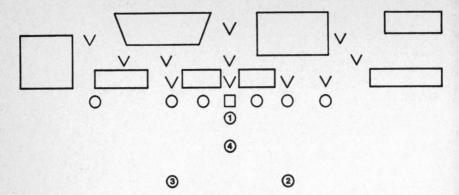

Diagram 9-13

Passing offense

1. Quick Pitch, HB Pass Left and Right.
2. Patterns 92-93.
3. Pattern 81.
4. Pattern 70, Hook and Slide 72.
5. Pattern 60-62.
6. Patterns 51-53-54-57.
7. Power 38 HB Pass.
8. Option Right Pass.

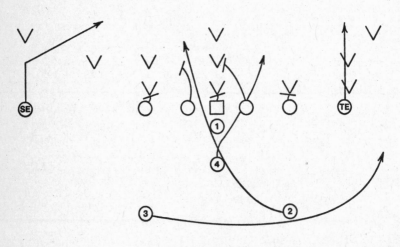

Diagram 9-14

Running against the 5-3 with the fullback usually makes the defensive tackle slant down. This is because of the quickness of the fullback and the good blocking angles of the guards. Diagram 9-14 shows Crossbuck 32-23.

Additional problems for the defense can be created by going to wide splits in the line. This provides more running room for the fullback and better blocking angles for linemen.

A change can occur in blocking up the middle against the 5-3 when the center can handle the nose guard by himself. As Diagram 9-15 shows, the middle linebacker is double teamed, and the center reverse cut-off blocks the middle guard away from the direction in which the fullback runs.

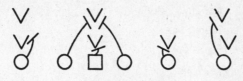

Diagram 9-15

If the defensive tackle slants inside, the offensive tackle's block should be an outside knee drive block or a reverse shoulder block. If the defensive man gets into the slant route before the blocker can stop his momentum, the tackle must drive block the lower legs to take away the defensive man's equilibrium.

The tackle slant will be difficult for the defense to use because of the Pro-Bone's halfback option. If the tackle is slanting down, the defensive end must come down hard inside to protect the open tackle area.

The tight end can drive block the lower legs of the defensive man or, if the defensive end is lined up on or inside shade, a quick pass block shielding the defensive man's penetration will open the second man option.

Furthermore, the quick pitch call will help keep the defensive end from slanting down hard.

6-1 Defense (Diagram 9-16)

Running offense

1. Lead Option Left and Right.
2. Option Left and Right.

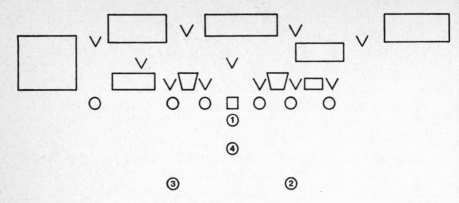

Diagram 9-16

3. Power 25-36 and 29-38.

4. 325-326 Reverses.

5. Tackle Trap.

6. Crossbuck 23-34.

7. Quarterback Sneak.

Passing offense

1. QB Power Rollouts Left and Right.

2. Pattern 93 (TE 10-yard post, SE 20-yard post).

3. Patterns 80-81.

4. Patterns 71-72 (Pattern 70, three back 10 yards and post).

5. Power 36-25 Halfback Pass.

6. Quick 52-54.

7. Option Right Pass.

8. 60 Series, FB Motion.

Against the 6-1, the Power 36 is a good off tackle play because the inside linebacker is far from the area being attacked. (Diagram 9-17.)

The halfback pass can also be used effectively because the defensive half is blocked by the two back coming out of the backfield each time. The two back can fake his block and then go upfield to take the pass from the other halfback. See Diagram 9-18.

When in the 6-1, it is also hard for the opposition to defense the halfback pass off the quick pitch. (Diagram 9-19.)

Since the 6-1 usually employs man-to-man coverage, three-man patterns out of the 60 or 90 series are successful, particularly

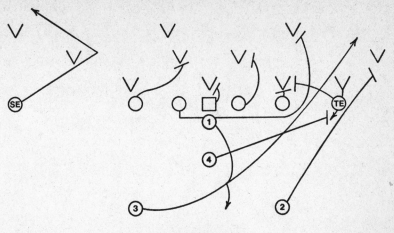

Diagram 9-17

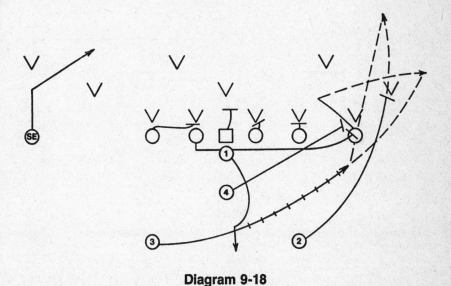

Diagram 9-18

with the halfback flaring out of the backfield. The linebacker cannot cover the outside area quickly enough.

6-2 Defense (Diagram 9-20)

Running offense

1. Power 25-26.
2. Quick Pitch 28-37.

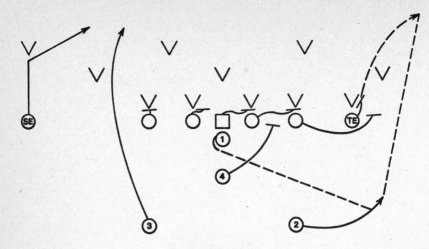

Diagram 9-19

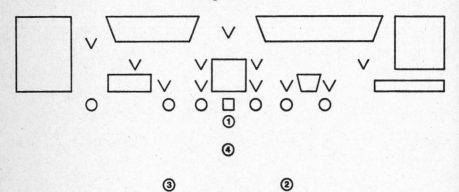

Diagram 9-20

3. Tackle Trap 13-14.

4. Lead Option, Pitch to HB.

5. QB Power Rollouts Left and Right.

6. Option Left and Right (HB handoff and pitch to outside).

Passing offense

1. Stand Up and Go.

2. Option Left HB Pass.

3. Patterns 92-94.

4. 70-72 Crossbuck.

5. 61-62.

6. 53-55.

7. Quick Pitch HB Pass.

8. 80 Series HB Motion.

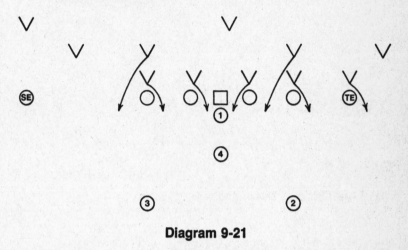

Diagram 9-21

The 6-2 is not usually a set defense. The linebackers (Diagram 9-21) can move out over the tackles and stunt.

The linebackers can also create a gap six, which is an eight-man front. Some defenses designate a strong linebacker to always cover and key, while the other moves anywhere on the line of scrimmage and stunts. The defensive linemen usually line up over, then shift to gap. See Diagram 9-22. This type of 6-2 should be blocked like a gap eight: The inside gap should be blocked and the linemen on the outside of the hole should block out.

Tackle traps from the weak side can be used to get more blocking in overloaded defensive areas.

Against the 6-2, draw plays and the quick hitting of the fullback can produce long gainers up the middle. Patience is a virtue against the 6-2; it can hold several downs in a row, then give up the big gain. The stand out pass to the split end and outside screens help

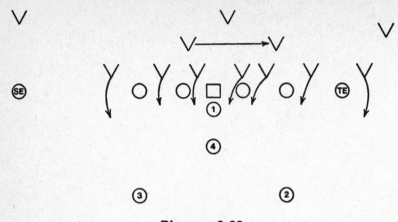

Diagram 9-22

take pressure off the quarterback. Flat areas are frequently open for the quick pass.

Goal Line Gap 8-3 Deep (Diagram 9-23)

Running offense

1. 23-34 Lead (wedge blocking in line).
2. 34-25 Sweep (line blocking first man to the inside).
3. Quick Pitch 28-37.
4. Crossbuck 23.
5. Tackle Trap.
6. 325-326 Reverses.

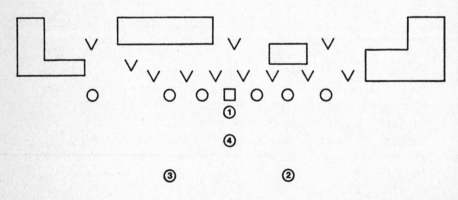

Diagram 9-23

Passing offense

1. Sweep 38 HB Pass.
2. 80 Series (RH motion, QB rollout right action).
3. Option Left HB Pass.
4. Quick Pitch HB Pass.
5. 53 All Hook, 55.
6. Option Right, Delayed Pass TE.

On the goal line—when the defense lines up in the gap eight, block down—trap out technique should be used. Wedge blocking should be used in the area of attack.

In this situation, an effective play off the 32 Power is the fake handoff and throw to either the tight end or split end. The split end fakes a block and runs a bench flag; the tight end a down and hook. See Diagram 9-24.

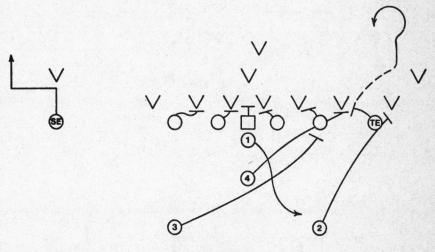

Diagram 9-24

Another good way of outmanning the eight-man front is to run the lead option with the fullback blocking the outside defensive man (Diagram 9-25).

Stacking Defense (Stunting) (Diagram 9-26)

Running offense

1. Option Right and Left (watch HB and pitch back).
2. Lead Option Right and Left.

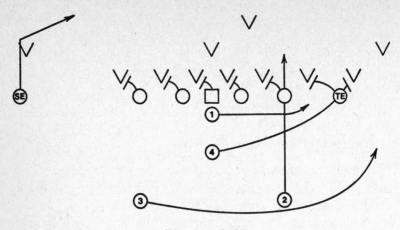

Diagram 9-25

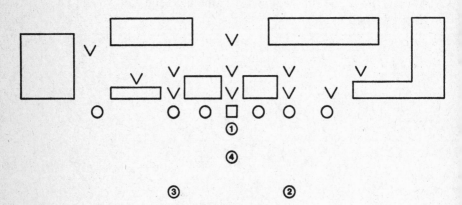

Diagram 9-26

3. Power Sweep 36-25 (line blocks down).

4. 23-34 Lead (wedge blocking).

5. Quick Pitches 28-37.

6. Power QB Rollouts (guards in).

Passing offense

1. Quick Pitch HB Pass.

2. Power QB Rollout Pass.

3. Option Right Pass TE.

4. Option Left and Right HB Pass.

5. 51-52-55-56.

A stacking, stunting defense should be blocked like a gap defense. The defense can't penetrate and all gaps are covered. A stacked defense also leaves outside areas open, making plays like quick pitches with the halfback pass particularly effective.

The following are pass patterns to be used against specific defensive secondary coverages. Note that the man to be covered is indicated above the defensive player.

Man-to-Man Coverage Three Deep (Diagram 9-27)

Pass patterns

1. Power 27-38 HB Pass.
2. Quick Pitch HB Pass.
3. Option Right or Left, HB Pass.
4. Pattern 92, HB Swing, Pattern 93.
5. Patterns 53-54.
6. 60-61 FB Motion.
7. 71-72.
8. 81.

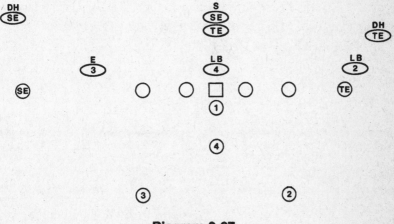

Diagram 9-27

Four Deep (Diagram 9-28)

Pass patterns

1. Power 36, 27 HB Pass.
2. Patterns 90-92 (weakside HB flares out of backfield after block).
3. Flea-Flicker.

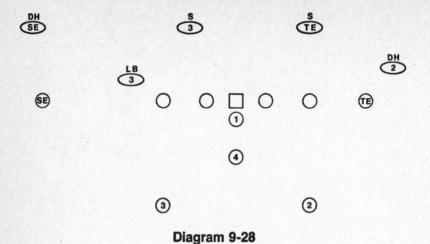

Diagram 9-28

4. 51-52-56.
5. 60-61 Motion.
6. 70.
7. 80-81.

Zone Coverage (Diagram 9-29—3 Deep, Diagram 9-30—4 Deep)

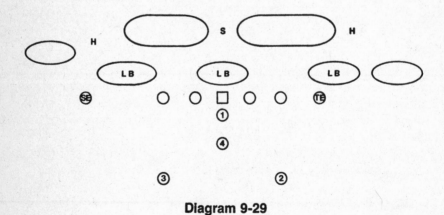

Diagram 9-29

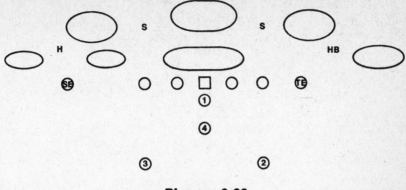

Diagram 9-30

Pass patterns

1. Power QB Rollout (flood pattern).
2. Option Left and Right (flood pattern).
3. Pattern 93 (fullback).
4. 72 Crossbuck.
5. 60 FB Motion, 61.
6. 51-52-57.
7. 81.
8. Quick Pitch HB Pass.

Such are the defenses and coverages that can be thrown against the Pro-Bone.

AFTERWORD

The Pro-Bone was designed for two main reasons. The first is the desire that is probably foremost in every coach's mind—the desire to try something new, to see his ideas acted out in a game situation where winning or losing identifies those ideas as acceptable or unacceptable. The second reason is more pragmatic: Defenses seem to have caught up to traditional offensive ideas.

As we have shown, the Pro-Bone will require some catching up to. Its key attribute is versatility. It involves a great deal for any defense to look at and adjust to.

As good as we think it is, the Pro-Bone is no more the "Ultimate Offensive System" than was the Single Wing or the Split T. We offer it as something for you to work with and add to, as an evolutionary phase in the game of football.

Index